GREAT
NORTHERNERS

GREAT
NORTHERNERS

ART BYRNE AND SEAN McMAHON

POOLBEG

A Paperback Original
First published 1991 by
Poolbeg Press Ltd
Knocksedan House,
Swords, Co. Dublin, Ireland.

Reprinted July, 1994

ISBN 1 85371 106 3

Cover design by Pomphrey Associates
Set by Richard Parfrey in ITC Stone
Printed by The Guernsey Press Co. Ltd Vale Guernsey
Channel Islands

For Richard Parfrey—a great Southerner

Introduction

Great Northerners is, as the title implies, a collection of
short lives of Ulster men and women who have a claim
to greatness. The name of Ulster is not automatically
associated with greatness: its image has for too many
years been one of death, violence and hate. Yet its sons
and daughters are as deserving of that epithet, great, as
those from any other comparable part of Ireland. For
historical reasons Ulster is the odd province, the contrary
region. Its clash of creed and race, the cause of its present
discontents, also produces a vitality, an inventiveness
and an energy that is and always has been extremely
creative. The province seems to have more than its share
of talent both aesthetic and technical. It has produced
generals for the British Army, inventions for agriculture
and industry, ships for the seven seas, hymns and popular
songs for the world to sing and its share of the customary
rich Irish contribution to the world of literature and
theatre. When last year we devised the book *Lives* we were
struck by the number of Ulster men and women who
qualified for inclusion. Since we had only limited space
and were forced to exclude many who deserved entry it
seemed appropriate to produce a book which would
celebrate the northern province in all its variety. These
hundred or so personalities are chosen without restriction
of creed, place or time. There are no "no-go" areas. Our
selection is as catholic and as representative as we could
make it but idiosyncrasy plays its part in all choice and

other compilers might have had different priorities. There is no *Dictionary of Ulster Biography*. Whether such an exclusive volume should exist or not is a political and not a bibliographical question. Yet the lives celebrated here and the many others which could not be included deserve to be placed on record. As the Bible, that Ulster bestseller, puts it, "Let us now praise famous men." Our century of lives is a first step in that praise.

Art Byrne and Sean McMahon, 1991

Contents

Cecil Francis Alexander 1

Harold Alexander 3

J B Armour 5

John Ballance 7

Sam Hanna Bell 9

Ernest Blythe 11

Patrick Brontë 13

Alan Brooke 15

Basil Brooke 17

Charlotte Brooke 19

Frances Browne 21

James Bryce.......................................23

Edward Bunting..................................25

Isaac Butt 27

William Carleton 30

Edward Carson 33

Roger Casement..................................35

James Caulfeild..................................38

Susannah Centilivre 40

Francis Chesney 42

Kitty Clive 44

John Colgan 46

Colum Cille 48

William Conor 50

Henry Cooke 52

James Craig...54

Francis Crozier...................................57

Joe Devlin...59

John Doherty......................................61

Lynn Doyle...63

Saumarez Dubourdieu 65

Charles Gavan Duffy 67
Johannes Duns Scotus 69
St John Ervine 71
George Farquhar 74
Brian Faulkner 76
Harry Ferguson 78
Sir Samuel Ferguson 80
Alec Foster 82
Vere Foster 84
Patrick Gallagher 86
Betsy Gray 89
Sir Tyrone Guthrie 91
Robert Hart 94
Hamilton Harty 96
Paul Henry 98
Frederick Hervey 100
May Hezlet 103
Bulmer Hobson 105
Jemmy Hope 108
John Hughes 110
Otto Jaffe 112
Patrick Kavanagh 114
Jimmy Kennedy 116
Sir John Lavery 118
Sean Lester 121
C S Lewis 123
Robert Lynd 126
Robert McCarrison 128
Henry Joy McCracken 130
Mary Ann McCracken 132
Somhairle Buí Mac Domhnaill 134
James McDyer 137
Albert McElroy 140
Patrick MacGill 142
Patrick McGilligan 145

Seosamh MacGrianna 147
Juan Mackenna 149
Charles Macklin 151
Heber MacMahon 153
Seumas MacManus 156
Louis MacNeice...............................158
Eóin MacNeill 160
St Malachy 163
Alice Milligan 165
Jane Verner Mitchel 167
John Mitchel 170
"Rinty" Monaghan 173
Micheál Ó Cléirigh 175
Peadar Ó Doirnín.............................177
Peadar O'Donnell 179
Tomás Ó Fiaich 182
Eoghan Rua Ó Neill 184
Hugh O'Neill...................................186
Terence O'Neill 189
Brian O'Nolan 192
Dehra Parker 194
Saidie Patterson 196
William Pirrie..................................199
Oliver Plunkett 202
Robert Lloyd Praeger.......................204
Amanda McKittrick Ros 206
Charles Russell 208
George Russell (Æ) 210
Philip Sheridan 212
Sir Hans Sloane 214
Robert Stewart, Lord Castlereagh 216
William Thomson, Baron Kelvin 218
John Toland 221
Helen Waddell 223
William Whitla 225

Cecil Francis Alexander

1818-95

Cecil Francis Alexander, the hymnist and poet, was born in Dublin in 1818, the daughter of Major John Humphreys of Wicklow, who on his appointment as land-agent to the Duke of Abercorn in 1833 brought his family to live in Milltown House, Strabane, Co Tyrone. As befitting an educated member of her class and sex she taught Protestant children in Sunday school and with a kindness uncharacteristic of the educational practice of the time tried to devise teaching methods appropriate to her charges. She attempted to make the catechetical year more interesting by writing seasonal verse. Her book *Hymns For Little Children* was published in 1848 and by some mysterious alchemy three of the pieces were wedded to tunes so appropriate that they became world famous. These were "All Things Bright and Beautiful" (originally known as "Septuagesima"), "There is a Green Hill Far Away" and "Once In Royal David's City" (printed as "Christmas.") In a sense, her literary life after that was something of an anticlimax, though her collected verse in *Poems* (1896) runs to 511 pages. She had, however, a full life as the wife of an ambitious clergyman who afterwards became Bishop of Derry. In 1851 she had married—late by the standards of the time—William Alexander, a rather "high" curate, six years younger than herself, and they had livings in Castlederg, Fahan and Strabane. In spite of the myriad duties of a rector's wife she still found time to write more verse and hymns. A long poem, "The Siege of Derry," describing the successful resistance of the city to the Jacobite armies from December 1688 till August 1689, was praised by Lord Macaulay, the classical historian of the period, and her imitation Border ballad "The Legend of Stumpie's Brae," set in a district across the river from her Co Tyrone girlhood home, is probably her most successful poem. In 1867 William Alexander became Bishop of Derry and Raphoe and the family went to live in the Bishop's palace within the walls of the siege city. It was the green hill of Creggan opposite the rear of this house that was the inspiration for her most famous hymn, "A Green Hill Far Away," one that the composer Gounod set, saying it was the most perfect in the English language. CFA (as she was known) died on 12 October 1895 and true to the high church practice accepted from her husband was, at her request, the first Protestant to have a cross as a memorial over her grave in the Derry cemetery. She is remembered in the city of her later years by a triptych stained-glass window in St Columb's Cathedral illustrating her three hymns, by a row of memorial cottages and by the plain white cross on another of the city's green hills.

Harold Alexander

1891-1969

Made Earl Alexander of Tunis, in memory of his 1943 victory which ended the German-Italian presence in North Africa, Harold Rupert Leofric Alexander was the third son of the fourth Earl of Caledon. He was born in London on 10 December 1891 but much of his childhood was spent at the family seat at Caledon, Co Tyrone. His father died in 1897 and his mother, Lady Elizabeth Graham-Toler, daughter of the third Earl of Norbury, was aloof and eccentric. Nevertheless Alexander was happy at Caledon and later at Harrow school where he loved athletics and art. From Sandhurst military college Alexander was commissioned into the appropriately aristocratic Irish Guards in 1911. Three years later he was in France where he fought all through the 1914-18 war; he was wounded twice, awarded the DSO and promoted rapidly from lieutenant to brigadier. The man who had originally intended leaving the army to become a painter was now in love with military life. In 1919 he was helping drive the Red army from Latvia and impressing his multinational brigade by the ease with which he learned both German and Russian. (Russia intrigued him and he was later an uncritical admirer of Stalin.) Alexander then came back to staff college and the command of the Irish Guards (1928-30). In the 1930s he served on the Indian north-west frontier with Auchinleck. On the outbreak of the 1939-45 war, Alexander was a divisional commander in France and took part in the retreat from

Dunkirk before the German onslaught. In 1942 he organised the retreat from Burma in the face of the Japanese advance. Despite such a negative career, Churchill had faith in Alexander and made him deputy to Eisenhower in North Africa. There he helped Montgomery to victory at Alamein before finally driving the Axis forces from North Africa at Tunis (1943). Alexander's amphibious assault on Sicily was successful but not quick enough to prevent the enemy withdrawal to the Italian mainland. Alexander then had to push his army northwards along the Italian peninsula. It was a secondary front to that of Normandy and so he was starved of troops. But he drove the Germans under Kesselring hard and they were obliged to withdraw troops from the Russian front to try to hold the line in Italy. In June 1944 Alexander took Rome. Now a field-marshal, but still spending more time forward than at his headquarters, thin, handsome and moustached, "Alex" was a hero to his men. At the end of the war, Alexander went to Canada as governor-general (1946-52) where he was happy and popular but perhaps not the best of diplomats, for his behaviour may have pushed John Costello, Taoiseach at the time, to announce Ireland's withdrawal from the Commonwealth at the Ottawa conference of 1949. Nor was Alexander happy as British Minister of Defence (1952-4) under his old (but still powerful) master, Churchill. His ghosted memoirs were published in 1962, but were not successful, being too disorganised and anecdotal. Alexander had married, in 1931, Lady Margaret Bingham, daughter of the fifth Earl of Lucan, by whom he had four children. He died after a heart attack on 16 July 1969 at Slough, and was buried near his home at Tyttenhanger, Hertfordshire.

J B Armour
1841-1928

The best known of all Ulster Presbyterian liberals, James Brown Armour was born on a farm at Lisboy, near Ballymoney, Co Antrim on 20 January 1841. He was one of six children of William Armour and Jane (née Brown). He was educated at Ballymoney Model, Royal Belfast Academical Institution, and at the Queen's colleges of Belfast and Cork, where he studied classics. Called to be minister of Second Ballymoney (Trinity) Presbyterian church (1869), he served the congregation until his retirement, being responsible for building both a new church and a lecture room. Armour had three sons by Jennie Stavely Hamilton, who had already been widowed with two sons when he married her (1883). Her brother-in-law, James MacMaster, professor of classics at Magee College, employed Armour as his part-time assistant lecturer (1885-1908). Politically, Armour followed the strong north Antrim tradition of supporting liberalism. When the Liberals decided to give home rule to Ireland, Armour was among those Liberal Unionists who joined with the Conservatives in opposition (1886). But he was unhappy, both with his new allies, who were mostly Church of Ireland, and with a unionism he saw as leading into a cul-de-sac. From 1893 he supported liberal Home Rulers for the north Antrim constituency in opposition to conservative Unionists. At the Presbyterian general-assembly, year after year, he spoke for the minority in his church who opposed Carsonite Unionism;

5

he argued that home rule would bring reconciliation with Catholics, increased trade and the end of the Church of Ireland's political monopoly. On the Liberals coming to power (1905), Armour was made chaplain to the Viceroy, Lord Aberdeen, with whom he had much influence. This he used to secure the appointment of liberals, like David Hogg and Lord Pirrie, as county lieutenants. Armour himself became a member of the senate of QUB, where he supported the introduction of scholastic philosophy and of Celtic studies, so as to attract Catholic students. Between 1912-22, Armour, now old and unwell, saw and deplored the Ulster unionist arming, the nationalist desertion of home rule for republicanism, and the partition of Ireland. His last political act was to help organise the meeting of Protestants who favoured home rule, at which Jack White, Roger Casement* and Alice Stopford Green spoke (Ballymoney, 24 October 1913). He died of pneumonia on 25 January 1928, having retired from the ministry three years before. He was mourned both by independent Presbyterians and by the Catholics ("A great light has gone out in Ulster," said Joe Devlin.*) "Armour of Ballymoney" (the title of the biography written by his son) became a mythical figure for nationalists on the lookout for Protestant supporters, no matter how few. But, for better or for worse, only a few Presbyterians accepted (or accept) his argument that unionism, "to spite the majority of our countrymen, sold its people into bondage, and through a senseless fear of Romanism, sacrificed the power and progress of true Presbyterianism in Ireland for generations" (speech to the Presbyterian special general-assembly at May Street Church, Belfast, March 1893).

John Ballance

1839-93

The prime minister known to New Zealanders as the "Rainmaker" was born on 27 March 1839, at Ballypitmave near Glenavy, Co Antrim, the eldest of eleven children of Samuel Ballance, a prosperous farmer, and of Mary (née McNeice), a Quaker. Educated at the local national school and at Wilson's Academy in Belfast, Ballance remained a great reader of history and of philosophy all his life. Having no interest in farming, he became an ironmonger's apprentice in Belfast, before emigrating, first to England where he was a hardware salesman in Birmingham (1857-66), and then to Wanganui in New Zealand. In Birmingham he had married Fanny Taylor and after her death in Wanganui he married Ellen Anderson, from Co Down. The couple had no children but adopted a niece, Kathleen. In Wanganui, Ballance established the *Evening Herald,* a newspaper which, though it made him little money, made him well-known in the area. Both his Irish background and his time in Birmingham had made him interested in politics. He was first elected to the General Assembly for Rangitikei (1875) and then for Wanganui (1879), which constituency he represented almost continuously until his death. He held office as colonial treasurer (1878), as minister of lands, native affairs and defence (1884-7) and as premier (1891-3). He was a radical liberal who refused a knighthood on principle. He believed in distributing land to encourage smallholder emigration, and in complete freedom of belief. He also campaigned for the vote for women, and tried to persuade the *Pakeha* (Europeans) to understand the Maori. He was not long enough in office to achieve all he wished but his reorganisation of the party and his determined attack on the conservative upper-house paved the way for the liberal triumphs of his successor, Seddon (1893-1912). He died of cancer on 27 April 1893, and was buried under an Irish granite headstone at Wanganui. Ballance followed Irish politics from a distance, and was a supporter both of tenant rights and of home rule—naturally enough for a man who encouraged his fellow colonials "to see themselves as New Zealanders rather than as Britons of the South Seas."

Sam Hanna Bell

1909-90

One of the finest of Ulster novelists, Sam Hanna Bell was born in Glasgow on 16 October 1909, but on the death of his father who worked as manager for the *Glasgow Herald* came "home" to live in Raffrey, near Crossgar, in Co Down. Later the family moved to Belfast. He had an almost American selection of jobs, including night-watchman, lab assistant and clerk for the Canadian Pacific Railroad. In the 1930s he was active in left-wing politics and during the war as a senior Civil Defence officer was put in charge of Belfast's emergency food supply. He began writing radio scripts for the BBC and short stories which were published in *The Bell*. These stories were later published as *Summer Loanen* in 1943 and are a kind of map of the imaginative Bell country in that the material and themes of his novels first appear in them. Louis MacNeice* was so impressed by his scripts that he appointed him to BBC Northern Ireland in 1945. He stayed there as Senior Features Producer till his retirement in 1969. He was responsible for many memorable programmes, and in a sense he discovered the playwright Sam Thompson. After his retirement he continued to write programmes especially for schools and became the editor of the Literary Miscellany feature of the *Ulster Tatler*. He died on 9 February 1990. Bell was the author of four novels, a book on Ulster folkways called *Erin's Orange Lily* (1956), a history of the theatre in Ulster (1972) and a prose anthology *Within Our Province*

(1972). His first and strongest novel, *December Bride* (1951), uniquely conveys the life of rural Protestant Ulster with its hard work, frugality, self-sufficiency and watchfulness. *The Hollow Ball* (1961), in a sense his only urban novel, is interesting in that it reflects the social and business life of Belfast in the 1930s and is unique in dealing with the left-wing movement of the time. It is also one of the few books written in Ireland that deals with the tough world of the professional footballer. *A Man Flourishing* (1973) combines the excitement of an historical romance with a marvellous account of the birthpangs of the industrial city, while his last novel *Across the Narrow Sea* (1987) is set in the Ulster of the plantation and has the humour, verve, sense of history and psychological accuracy of all his work. Sadly he did not live to see a special private showing of the film of *December Bride* which was completed in the spring of 1990.

Ernest Blythe

1889-1975

In turn journalist, revolutionary, cabinet minister, theatre manager, Ernest Blythe was born at Magheragall, Lisburn, Co Antrim on 13 April 1889. The eldest child of James and Agnes Blythe, he was educated at Maghaberry national school before becoming a boy clerk with the department of agriculture in Dublin in 1905. In a first volume of autobiography, *Trasna na Bóinne* (1957), he recalled going to Irish classes given by Sinéad Flanagan (later Mrs de Valera) and being recruited into the Irish Republican Brotherhood by Seán O'Casey. Moving to Newtownards in 1909, he wrote unionist editorials for the *North Down Herald* on which he worked (and with whose policy it was assumed he, as a Protestant, was in agreement), helped the local dramatic society produce *The Drone*, and recruited for the IRB. Realising that only by living in a Gaeltacht area could he perfect his Irish, he moved in 1913 to Cinn Ard near Lispole in Co Kerry where he worked as a farmhand for Gregory Ashe. He recalled that period later, in his second volume of autobiography, *Slán le hUltaibh* (1970): how he made the family speak Irish to him by refusing to notice anything said in English; how he translated and produced a play by Yeats; how he met Desmond FitzGerald (married to Mabel McConnell from Donaghadee) who lent him French novels to read; and how he fell in love with Kerry. From 1914 Blythe was actively involved in the revolutionary movement; during the 1916 insurrection he was out of Dublin but was imprisoned after the rebels surrendered. In 1918 he was elected for Sinn Féin in North Monaghan and became minister for trade in the first Dáil Eireann in 1919. In 1922 he took the pro-treaty side, becoming finance minister in the new Free State government. Holding the office until 1932, he was enormously influential; it was Blythe who kept the civil service system inherited from the British, who forced the army to accept a cut of 15,000 men, who doggedly negotiated a new financial relationship with Britain, who backed the Shannon hydro-electric scheme against the advice of his own department. Blythe lost his seat in the 1933 election but he remained in politics until 1936 as a member of the senate. Blythe had never lost his interest in the theatre; in 1924 he granted the Abbey its first subsidy and he had encouraged the setting up of the Taibhdhearc in Galway. So it was not surprising that he became a member of the Abbey's board in 1935 and its managing director in 1941. While in charge at the Abbey he was accused of employing only Gaelic-speaking actors and of favouring box-office kitchen comedies at the expense of new plays. But since his retirement in 1967 critics have become more aware of his achievements: holding the company together at the Queen's Theatre after the disastrous fire at the Abbey in 1951 and then extracting from the government enough money to build a completely new theatre. In 1919 Blythe had married Annie McHugh, by whom he had one son. Though he continued to live in Dublin until his death on 23 February 1975, Blythe never lost a black Northern sense of fun: on his way home from giving a talk in Belfast in which he had praised the Northern government, he was called a "Presbyterian bastard" by an irate republican. "Wrong on both counts," retorted Blythe and walked on.

Patrick Brontë

1777-1861

Patrick Brontë, the father of the Brontë sisters, was born
on St Patrick's Day 1777, the son of a Protestant father,
Hugh Prunty, and a Catholic mother. The ruin of the
cottage where he was born at Emdale, Ballynaskeagh, Co
Down has a tourist plaque commemorating the event.
The family was poor but like many of the time and place
respectful of learning and the church. He was apprenticed
to a weaver at the age of fifteen but had hankerings after
a formal education which was supplied by the Rev
Andrew Harshaw who taught the boy classics. This
instruction was supplemented by Prunty's own
determination to learn, a zeal which caused him to rise
at four o'clock in the morning to study. He became the
teacher in a school in Drumgooland, not far from his
home, but had to give it up because of a scandal involving
one of his pupils. The offence was venial and the affection
reciprocated but it meant the end of his teaching career.
He was taken up by the local Church of Ireland clergyman,
the Rev Mr Tighe, who, supplementing Harshaw's work,
enabled the talented, if morose young man to gain a
scholarship to St John's College, Cambridge in 1802.
There he changed the spelling of his name to Brontë and
on graduation found a number of livings as a curate in
Essex, Wellington and Dewsbury. He led a frugal life and
managed to send £20 home to his mother each year
during her lifetime. In 1812 he married a Cornish girl,
Maria Branwell, and in 1820 with six children became

the permanent curate at Haworth, a weaving village on the edge of the Yorkshire moors. He had published two volumes of simple verse about the time of his marriage with predictable titles, *Cottage Poems* (1811) and *The Rural Minstrel* (1812). His wife died of cancer in 1821 and her sister Aunt Branwell, a strict Methodist, helped him rear the children. His two eldest children, Maria and Elizabeth, died at the school which was later written about as Lowood, and Charlotte's health never recovered from the conditions there. As a father he was remote, strict but not unappreciative of his four remaining highly talented children. He could be difficult. Once he burned the children's boots because he fancied they were showing off in them; a silk dress of his wife suffered the same fate. The children were vegetarian by default since no meat was ever served to them. His favourite daughter was Maria, the eldest, who died when she was eleven. They used read the newspaper together and discuss current affairs. He remained outwardly calm at his son Branwell's drunken bouts and his scandalous amatory involvements and he bore the deaths of all his talented children with stoicism. He retained too his Ulster egalitarianism, especially in his support of striking Yorkshire weavers. And most characteristically he preserved the literary relics of his children with quiet pride. Charlotte was the last to die. She lived at Haworth, tending her father's steadily deteriorating eyesight and finally overcoming his opposition to her marrying his curate, the Rev George Bell Nicholls, in 1854. She died of a chill after the birth of her child in 1855. Her father survived till 7 June 1861.

Alan Brooke

1883-1963

The military adviser in whom Winston Churchill placed most trust during the 1939-45 war, Alan Francis Brooke, was born at Bagnères-de-Bigorre (Pyrénées) on 23 July 1883. He was the ninth child of Sir Victor Brooke of Colebrook, Co Fermanagh, and of Alice Sophia Bellingham, who lived in a flourishing English-speaking colony at Pau for most of the year save in high summer when they moved to the cooler foothills of the Pyrénées. At Pau, Brooke was educated at the Lycée St-George together with his nephew Basil* who was four years younger. Considered too delicate for the rigours of a British public school, Brooke did not leave his mother (who was widowed in 1891) until at eighteen he entered the Royal Military Academy at Woolwich. A military career was inevitable in a family which had helped Elizabeth I conquer Ireland in the sixteenth century (and would send twenty-six members to fight against Germany in the 1914-18 war). Brooke saw service with an artillery regiment in Ireland from 1902 and in India from 1906. In the 1914-18 war he was the first British artilleryman to use the French idea of a "creeping barrage" between advancing infantry and the enemy trenches. Awarded the DSO, Brooke attended staff college (1919-21) and returned there as instructor (1923-7) before commanding the artillery school, and then, in 1935, an infantry brigade. He believed, naturally for a gunner who had served in the 1914-18 war, that firepower dominated movement in modern warfare. But by the time he became director of military training at the War Office, he was more sympathetic to military theorist Liddell Hart's idea that mechanisation would restore movement to the battlefield. Serving with the British force in France in 1940, he criticised both the force commander, Lord Gort's, leadership and French morale and advised the British government to withdraw. After the retreat from Dunkirk he became commander of home forces and, in 1941, Chief of Imperial General Staff. As CIGS, Brooke worked most successfully with the naval and air force commanders, Cunningham and Portal. He advised Churchill to promote Alexander* and Montgomery, two very able British commanders and both with Anglo-Irish backgrounds. He accompanied Churchill to the inter-Allied conferences at Casablanca, Quebec and Moscow in 1943 where the strategy which eventually defeated the Germans and Italians was decided. Brooke worked hard to ensure a good relationship with the American allies, though he was rather hurt when Eisenhower became, inevitably, the supreme allied commander. Above all, Brooke channelled Churchill's genius and ensured it was never misdirected towards unsound strategic schemes. He found Churchill very difficult but "would not have missed working with [him] for anything on earth." A field-marshal since 1944, he became Baron (later Viscount) Alanbrooke of Brookeborough (1945) and retired from the army in 1946. In 1949 he became chancellor of Queen's University, Belfast. Rapid of thought and speech in public, in private Brooke was a gentle man and a devoted ornithologist. He married Jane Mary Richardson of Ballinamallard in 1914 and, after her death in a motoring accident in 1925, Benita Lees (née Pelly), a widow. Alanbrooke died at his home in Hartley Wintney, Hampshire on 17 June 1963.

Basil Brooke
1888-1973

The first of five children of Douglas Brooke and Gertrude
Isabella (née Batson of Cambridgeshire), Basil Brooke
was born on 9 June 1888 at Colebrooke, Co Fermanagh,
on an estate which had been awarded to an ancestor
from Cheshire who had served in Elizabeth I's army.
Brooke was educated at Pau, where his grandparents
lived among an English-speaking colony, and at
Winchester, which he found academically too demand-
ing. Following a long tradition of "fighting Brookes," he
went to Sandhurst and, after being commissioned, served
in India with the Royal Fusiliers and later with the 10th
Hussars. In the 1914-18 war, after a short period in the
trenches, he became *aide-de-camp* to General Byng, and
helped interpret in negotiations with Marshal Foch. At
war's end Brooke retired from the army, married Cynthia
Mary Surgison from Sussex, and returned to Colebrooke
which, since his father's death in 1907, had been run by
his alcoholic mother. Good farming practice soon
improved the estate but the condition of the Ireland to
which he had returned was much more difficult. After
the 1916 insurrection he "refused to describe [himself] as
an Irishman" and to combat disloyalty pioneered the
local special constabulary, an almost completely
Protestant force, of which he became Fermanagh
commandant. While in Dublin for his wife's confinement
in 1920, he was shocked at the collapse of British rule. In
the new Northern Ireland which emerged from the

settlement of 1920-1, he went into politics, as county councillor (1924) and as MP (1929) for the carefully created unionist divisions of Brookeborough and Lisnaskea. A *protégé* of Prime Minister James Craig*, Brooke was a successful minister of agriculture (1933-41). As minister of production he showed himself one of the few ministers able to adjust to wartime (1939-45) pressures, and so became prime minister (1943) in succession to the geriatric JM Andrews. After the war, in which he lost two sons, Brooke led the Unionists to a begrudging acceptance of socialist reforms in health and education decreed by Westminster. In 1949, when the Free State declared itself a republic, he persuaded the British government to restate Northern Ireland's position within the UK. Brooke was easily able to deal with the 1956 IRA campaign because it lacked support from the Catholic population. In 1963, when he retired, he could reasonably claim that Ulster was the most prosperous part of Ireland. On the other hand he had hardly altered his view, expressed at an Orange demonstration in 1933, that Catholics desired "the destruction of Ulster," and this was to leave Terence O'Neill, his successor as prime minister, with an almost impossible task in his attempts at reconciliation. When Lord Brookeborough (as he had become in 1952) died at Colebrooke, on 18 August 1973, the Northern Ireland political system had already collapsed. For this he was blamed, both by the preacher at his memorial service, who lamented that "throughout his time as prime minister, the barriers between Protestant and Roman Catholic were virtually unbreached," and by many obituary writers. On the other hand, Brooke was remembered by many disillusioned unionists as the man who had presided over a golden age of stability.

Charlotte Brooke

c.1740-93

Charlotte Brooke, the author and Gaelic scholar, was born in Rantavan, Co Cavan, about the year 1740. She was the only one of twenty-two children of Henry Brooke, the playwright and novelist, to survive her father's death. He had earned a reputation in London because of a play, *Gustavus Vasa,* based on the life of the Protestant king of Sweden who held the country for the Reformation. Charlotte, "the child of his old age," was very clever and her father supervised her education at home in Cavan. The family moved to Killybegs near Naas and the proximity to Dublin and the theatre caused a crisis in her life. She became obsessed by the stage; she wrote a play for the Smock Alley company on the Earl of Essex and became friendly with the great David Garrick and his companion Peg Woffington and even considered acting as a profession. This preoccupation ended with her mother's illness. She returned home to nurse her and after she died became her father's housekeeper. With much enforced leisure and her interest in the stage in abeyance she took up Irish and learned Old, Middle and Modern Irish so successfully that she decided to translate some of the old texts into English. Her first effort was the translation of a monody by Carolan which was published anonymously in Joseph Walker's *Historical Memoirs of the Irish Bards* (1786), and she went on to publish a number of translations mainly of old texts. These were printed with the Irish texts as *Reliques of Ancient Irish*

Poetry in 1787. Her father had died in 1783 and due either to the incompetence or malfeasance of a friend she lost the money that was to have been her mainstay. Applications made by the Earl of Charlemont* on her behalf to the Royal Irish Academy for a post as chatelaine were rejected, to her intense mortification, but she earned enough from the subscription publication of the *Reliques* and an edition of her father's extensive works to enable her to buy a competent annuity. She did not, however, survive to enjoy it for long, dying on 29 March 1793 in Longford. Her work in directing people's attention to the Irish texts is more significant than the quality of her translations. Her interest in the poetry "couched in an almost obsolete language" helped to counteract the plain fact that in the words of her introduction, "The British muse is not yet informed that she has an elder sister in this isle." The *Reliques*, like Percy's *Reliques of Ancient English Poetry* (1765), acted as a spur to the growth of romanticism in English literature and helped keep the literary tradition of Gaelic Ireland sufficiently alive until its own renaissance in the next century. Her name is also associated with what her memoirist perhaps inaccurately calls *Bolg tSolair*, the earliest Irish language magazine which had its sole number published in Belfast in 1795.

Frances Browne

1816-79

Frances Browne, known popularly as "the blind poetess of Donegal," was born in Stranorlar on 16 January 1816, the daughter of the local postmaster. Blind from infancy as a result of smallpox, she was nevertheless sent to the local school, run by a Mr McGranahan, where one of her fellow-pupils was Isaac Butt*. She learned by listening to the other children saying their lessons and with the aid of a deliberately developed and prodigious memory soon became very well-read, with an abiding love of English literature. She began writing poetry as a child and her first poem, sent in without her knowledge by a friend, appeared in the Belfast *Northern Whig.* Later work was published in the *Irish Penny Journal,* in *Hood's Magazine* and the *Athenaeum.* Her best known poem, "Songs of Our Land" with its stirring peroration—"Still hearts that are bravest and best of the nations/ Shall glory and live in the songs of their land!"—appeared in the *Journal* on 6 March 1841. Her first collection *The Star of Atteghei,* published in 1844, so impressed Sir Robert Peel that he obtained for her an annual £20 pension from the Civil List. This confirmed in her a determination to live by her writing. She and her sister who acted as an amanuensis went to Edinburgh in 1847 to further her career. Here she met John Wilson, the often abusive and right-wing professor of moral philosophy at the university who as "Christopher North" wrote *Noctes Ambrosianae* and was one of the most influential literary figures in the northern capital. He adopted her, introduced her to his circle and found work for her in *Chambers's Magazine*. She was a tireless worker, turning out articles, poems, stories and reviews. Some of her most popular writing was her retelling of Ulster legends for Irish newspapers. Her second collection, *Lyrics and Miscellaneous Poems*, was published in 1848 and dedicated to her patron Peel. Another benefactor, the Marquis of Landsdowne, gave her £100 which enabled her to move to London and continue a full social and literary life. She died on 25 August 1879 of a heart complaint. Her best-known work was a collection of fairy stories, *Granny's Wonderful Chair and the Stories It Told*, published in 1857 and an instant bestseller. It went out of print eventually but had a second life when Frances Hodgson Burnett, the famous children's author, published twenty years later *Stories from the Lost Fairy Book as Retold by the Child who Read Them*. The stories were reprinted in the children's anthology, *The Lucky Bag* (Dublin:1984).

James Bryce

1838-1922

Liberal politician and writer, James Bryce was born at Arthur Street, Belfast on 10 May 1838. His father, after whom he was named, was a schoolmaster and geologist who had married Margaret Young, the daughter of a Belfast merchant. After a happy childhood, much of it spent at Abbeyville, his grandfather's house outside Belfast, Bryce went to school at Glasgow High School (where his father taught from 1846) and then, in 1852, to Belfast Academy, where his uncle Reuben was principal. Afterwards Bryce studied classics, history and law at Glasgow University, at Trinity College, Oxford (to which he won a scholarship) and at Heidelberg. Bryce practised at the bar for a short period and in a very gentlemanly fashion before becoming regius professor of civil law at Oxford in 1870. In *Transcaucasia and Ararat* (1877), Bryce described a journey to Russia and Armenia, from which he returned a supporter of Armenia, in opposition to the prime minister, Disraeli, who backed the Turkish Empire. Bryce entered politics as a Liberal, and was elected to parliament for Tower Hamlets in 1880 and then for South Aberdeen (1885-1906). Bryce was too learned a speaker to be successful in parliament, and, though he sat in three cabinets, he never gave all of his energies to politics. In 1886 he was under-secretary for foreign affairs in Gladstone's short-lived government; in 1892 he helped Gladstone's new cabinet prepare the Irish Home Rule Bill, before chairing a commission which recommended greater involvement by central government in secondary education. When the Liberals were rejected by the electorate in 1895, Bryce resumed travelling and writing. He had already published *The American Commonwealth* (1888) and now he gave his *Impressions of South Africa* (1897). The volume was nicely timed to allow Bryce to pose as an expert critic of the Conservative government's handling of the war against the Boers. But Bryce's limitations as a practical politician were shown in 1905 when he became Irish chief secretary: he underestimated the strength of feeling in favour of Home Rule and he failed to settle the university question. He was sent as British ambassador to Washington (1907-13) where he was popular because of his earlier writings and because of his Presbyterian democratic directness. In the Lords, as Viscount Bryce, he supported the 1914 bill excluding Ulster from the home rule settlement. During the 1914-18 war he produced a report on alleged German terrorism in Belgium, and, with ex-president Taft of the USA, a plan for a post-war league of nations. In 1921 he published his last book, *Modern Democracies*, and gave his last speech in the Lords (in support of the adoption of the Anglo-Irish treaty). Bryce died at Sidmouth on 22 January 1922 and was buried in Edinburgh. He died a fellow of the Royal Society (1893), a foreign member of the Institut de France (1904), honoured by thirty-one universities. He had married Elizabeth Marion Ashton of Didsbury in 1889.

Edward Bunting

1773-1843

Edward Bunting, the first great collector of Irish traditional music, was born in Armagh in 1773, the son of an Irish mother and an English father who was a mining engineer. After his father's death, Bunting went to live with his brother Anthony who was an organist in Drogheda (1782). At the age of eleven, he became assistant organist to Mr Ware at St Anne's, Belfast. For the next thirty years "Atty" Bunting lodged with the McCracken family and was a firm friend of both Mary Ann* and Henry Joy*, though he never showed any interest in their revolutionary politics. Appointed musical scribe to the gathering of traditional harpers, which the enlightened and patriotic bourgeoisie of the expanding city had organised in the assembly room of Belfast exchange, 1792, Bunting became interested in Irish music and published sixty-six airs in his *General Collection of the Ancient Irish Music* (1796). To collect more tunes, Bunting visited, at Magilligan, Denis Hempson, the last harpist to play *ar an sean-nós* with long crooked finger-nails. Bunting also travelled to Connacht with Richard Kirwan, and later with Patrick Lynch, who could copy down and translate the Gaelic words of the traditional songs. Bunting published the results of this itinerant collecting in *A General Collection of the Ancient Music of Ireland* (1809), after which he ceased travelling, though he did publish a third collection, *Ancient Music of Ireland,* in 1840. Bunting's collections help our knowledge both of the traditional harper's methods of playing and of the airs themselves. But he was not always an accurate scribe; after noting "The Princess Royal" from Arthur O'Neill, he then published the tune in F minor, a key in which an Irish harpist could not have played. And, in an attempt to compete with Thomas Moore, who had borrowed tunes from the 1796 collection, Bunting, rather than use Lynch's translations of the originals, had Campbell and other versifiers write new words for the traditional airs. The 1809 collection made Bunting famous, especially in Belfast where he was musical director of the Harp Society (1808-13) and where he conducted the first local performance of Handel's *Messiah* at the Second Presbyterian Church. A portly, sophisticated, rather lazy bachelor, Bunting at last married in 1819, a Miss Chapman, and moved to Dublin as organist at St Stephen's, Mount Street. A visiting Belfast friend was advised by Mrs McTier, who knew Bunting well, to bring "sweetys, his greatest temptation, for he despises both money and praise." Bunting continued to correspond with the McCrackens in Belfast and even brought his son and two daughters north to visit them. He died in 1843 and is buried in Mount Jerome cemetery.

Isaac Butt

1813-79

Isaac Butt, the founder and namer of the Home Rule movement, was born at Cloghan, Co Donegal on 6 September 1813. His father was a Church of Ireland clergyman who ministered in Stranorlar in that county. Butt was educated at the Royal School, Raphoe and at Trinity College, Dublin where he had an outstanding academic career. He published translations of Virgil and Ovid by the time he was twenty-one. One of the founders of the *Dublin University Magazine*, he served as its editor from 1834 till 1838. He became professor of political economy in 1836 but abandoned the academic life in 1841 for the greater excitement and richer pickings of the bar. He soon became as famous at pleading as his great rival Daniel O'Connell, against whom he engaged in public debate as the voice of conservatism and defender of Protestant ascendancy. This led to his writing for the conservative press in England and the founding of a Dublin weekly newspaper called the *Protestant Guardian*. It was the great famine of the Forties and England's inadequate response to the catastrophe that changed his mind about the Union, and his legal career afterwards was dominated by his defence of nationalists, notably Smith O'Brien in the late 1840s and the Fenians two decades later. This acquaintance with the aims and ideals of the militants was one of the causes of the arch-conservative becoming liberal. It led to a political career based upon the belief that with some federal association of Ireland and Britain instead of the unworkable union lay the best solution to the perennial Irish Question. His Home Government Association became the Home Rule League in 1873 and in the general election of 1874 he was returned as member for Limerick and head of a party which had won half the Irish seats in the House of Commons. However, his extreme constitutionalism and reluctance to embarrass the government caused his supporters to grow impatient. Joseph Biggar, the Belfast MP and member of the Irish Republican Brotherhood, who was to prove so effective a deputy for Butt's successor, had already begun to apply the tactics of obstructionism that eventually produced results. Butt never lost a sense of respect for Britain and thought it ungentlemanly for the Irish party to use tactics which were intended to bring legislation to a standstill. By the time of the Balkan Crisis of 1878 the divergence of opinion between the old leader and the young men on his heels was made very clear. Butt thought that at such a time of "national" emergency responsible men had a duty to support the British government, whereas John Dillon wanted the Home Rule party to leave the House *en masse* to make clear their lack of community of interest with Britain in her overseas affairs. Butt was effectively dismissed in February 1879 and the way was clear for Parnell to make the Home Rule party the most effective and best organised parliamentary caucus ever devised. Butt died on 5 May of that year and was buried in Stranorlar. His personal life was not free from troubles: minor scandals dogged his career and he served an eighteen-month sentence in Dublin for debt. His conversion to nationalism was never complete and his gentlemanly gradualism was too radical for his Protestant friends and too ineffective for Catholics. Yet his courage in rejecting the cosy conservatism of his early life is entirely commendable and it is clear that his Home Rule agitation paved the way for the successes which followed under more dynamic and more ruthless leaders.

William Carleton

1794-1869

William Carleton, the truest portrayer of the poor
nineteenth-century Irish peasantry, was born on 4 March
1794 in the townland of Prillisk in the Clogher valley of
Co Tyrone. His mother was Gaelic-speaking and knew
many of the old Irish songs and traditional poems. His
father was an under-tenant and a man of prodigious
memory. His son recalled, "As a teller of old tales,
legends, and historical anecdotes he was unrivalled, and
his stock of them was inexhaustible." The family was
bilingual, and with such a store of domestic knowledge
and the rough but thorough education of the hedge-
schools the young Carleton was well placed to become
the laureate of his people. He first considered becoming
a priest, though the style of rural life of the period with
plentiful illicit liquor and the pre-Famine lack of
puritanism was not an ideal preparation for orders. As he
put it in the introduction to one of his published volumes:
"I attended every wake, dance, fair and merry-making in
the neighbourhood and became so celebrated for dancing
hornpipes, jigs and reels, that I was soon without a rival
in the parish." The stories which he wrote and which
were later published as *Traits and Stories of the Irish
Peasantry* (1830) are practically autobiographical. The
almost medieval richness and crudity of Irish life at the
time, the dissoluteness and violence of some of the
hedge-schoolmasters whose services were so important
to the ambitious peasantry, his own crisis of conscience,

which led during a pilgrimage to Lough Derg to his decision not to go to Maynooth as a clerical student—all are portrayed with great truth in the stories. His account of the Ribbonmen, whose society he joined for a time in his youth, is starkly authentic. After he rejected the idea of becoming a priest he became a wandering tutor and finally reached Dublin. There he fell under the influence of the fanatical Protestant Caesar Otway who recognised from the young Tyrone man's conversation a talent which would find its shape and discipline in writing. His early work was published in Otway's periodical, the *Christian Examiner.* About this time he married a Protestant girl, Jane Anderson and happily joined her church. Otway wanted Carleton to provide proof of the old Protestant charge of Popish abominations and superstitions but Carleton's sketches took on a life of their own as literature and failed in their propaganda purpose. He lived in Dublin for the rest of his life writing for anyone who would employ him. His five-year sojourn with the *Examiner* (1826-1831) had made his name known to such sympathetic and influential people as Maria Edgeworth. She had a hand in his receiving a Civil List pension of £200 a year but even his acceptance of this was regarded as further proof of his venality and renegadism. What his detractors did not understand was that Carleton was the ideal reflector of the Irish peasant because he remained at heart an under-tenant whose purpose was survival, care of his family and patch and avoidance of the connected evils of poverty and eviction. His dark reaction to the Great Hunger of the 1840s, of which he is the starkest recorder, exemplifies this. The experiences of his youth which included drink, womanising, secret societies and earlier famines provided him with the material for the many novels he continued to write until five years before he died. These include

Valentine M'Clutchy (1845), an excoriation of the landlord class, and *The Black Prophet* (1847), a powerful tale of the Famine. His *Autobiography* remained unfinished when he died in Dublin on 30 January 1869.

Edward Carson

1854-1935

An able lawyer but a man too idealistic to be a successful politician, Edward Henry (Ned) Carson was born in Dublin, 9 February 1854, one of six children of Edward Carson, a Dublin architect, and of Isabella Lambert of Castle Ellen, Co Galway. Following education at boarding school in Portarlington and at TCD, where he took an undistinguished degree in classics, he was called to the bar from King's Inns (1877). After practising on the Leinster circuit, he became crown-prosecutor (he was nicknamed "Coercion" Carson for his prosecution of the Land League). Elected Liberal-Unionist MP for Dublin University, he moved to London and began to make a name at the English bar. His technique of cross-examination was famous (in the Oscar Wilde case, Carson shook the eloquent playwright by suddenly asking "Did you kiss him?") With his enormous earnings, he kept houses in London and at Rottingdean, where he lived with his wife (Annette Kirwan from Co Galway) and four children. After his first wife's death, he married Ruby Frewen, half his age, by whom he had a son when he was already a sixty-six year old grandfather. Carson was notoriously hypochondriacal and spent long periods convalescing, at home in bed or at Bad Homburg, the German spa. Politics brought Carson advancement—by 1900 he was Solicitor-General for England and had been knighted—but his later political involvement was chiefly motivated by his desire to keep Ireland united to Britain.

As leader of Irish unionism (1910), he encouraged Craig*
and the Ulster Unionists in their stand against Home
Rule. He spoke at public meetings throughout unionist
Ulster, as well as in Liverpool and Glasgow, on the week
the Covenant was signed (September 1912). He supported
gun-running and the establishment of a provisional
government in Ulster. During the war of 1914-18 (which
postponed an Irish settlement) Carson was in turn
Attorney-General, in charge of the navy, and finally in
the war cabinet. MP for Duncairn (1918), he welcomed
the establishment of Northern Ireland but bitterly
condemned the giving of independence to the rest of
Ireland. To a friend he declared, "the Celts have done
nothing in Ireland but create trouble." Carson's final
years were spent as a law lord (1921-9) and, more
happily, with his young wife and child in their new
home, Thanet. On his death (22 October 1935) Carson
was given a naval funeral to St Anne's cathedral, Belfast,
where he was buried. Prime Minister Craigavon spoke for
all Ulster Unionists in his broadcast tribute: "...by the
working-class of this province he was adored."

Roger Casement

1864-1916

Roger David Casement was born in Dublin, 1 September 1864, one of four children of Roger Casement, a British army officer from Co Antrim, and of Anne (née Jephson, of a Catholic collateral branch of the Munster Anglo-Irish family.) When his mother died in childbirth, 1873, and his father soon afterwards, Casement became the ward of his uncle, John, at Magherintemple house, near Ballycastle, Co Antrim. After an education at what is now Ballymena Academy, he went to Liverpool where an aunt got him a job in the Elder Dempster Shipping Co. His work brought him to Africa where he remained to serve a Belgian exploration company in the Congo and then a British company in Nigeria (1884-95). Having joined the British consular service, he was stationed in Portugese West Africa and then in the Belgian Congo (where his reports condemned native enslavement). Home on leave in 1904, he became involved in nationalist circles and with Ada McNeill, Bulmer Hobson* and Alice Stopford Green, organised the Cushendall feis. To learn Gaelic, he went to Cloghaneely, Co Donegal in 1907. Meanwhile he had been posted to Brazil where he served as consul at Santos (1906), at Belem (1908), and as consul-general at Rio de Janeiro (1909). There he inquired into the misbehaviour of the Peruvian Amazon Co towards its Indian rubber-gatherers. Casement's Putumayo Report (1912) led to the condemnation of the British directors of the rubber company. For his work,

Casement had already been knighted in 1911 (an honour he accepted as an anti-slavery campaigner but disliked as an Irish nationalist). Having, in 1913, resigned from the consular service after nearly thirty years in the tropics, he became deeply involved in nationalist activity: speaking at Ballymoney (October 1913); helping plan the running of guns to Howth (1914); going to the USA as a nationalist propagandist. There he met the German ambassador, von Bernstorff, who invited him to visit Germany. Accompanied by a Norwegian companion, who was in the pay of British intelligence, Casement went to Berlin (1914). Casement visited the Irish prisoners-of-war at Limburg and tried to win them from their British allegiance, but they were not impressed by his upper-class accent nor by his romanticism. When the Germans sent 20,000 rifles on board the *Aud* to help the insurrection planned in Ireland (Easter 1916), Casement joined the U-boat escort. The expedition was a fiasco and Casement was lucky not to have drowned before being arrested at Banna strand and imprisoned in Tralee, Co Kerry, RIC barracks (Good Friday 1916). Taken to London under guard, he was lodged in the Tower and charged with treason. Bernard Shaw wrote to Casement advising him to claim that as an Irish nationalist, he was entitled to prisoner-of-war status; but Casement's counsel, Alexander Sullivan, preferred to argue about the definition of treason in the 1351 act. Casement was found guilty, immediately stripped of his knighthood, and sentenced to be hanged on 3 August 1916. Before death he took the Catholic sacraments; he had already been baptised secretly as a child by his mother. Casement's diaries, which showed he was an active homosexual, were circulated privately by the British government to discredit him and prevent his becoming a martyr. When Casement's bones were allowed back to Ireland for burial (1965), not in his beloved Antrim but at Glasnevin, playwright David Rudkin saw in him, as outsider both politically and sexually, a symbol of the modern Ulster Protestant (in *Cries from Casement as his Bones are Brought to Dublin*, broadcast by the BBC in 1973).

James Caulfeild, Earl of Charlemont
1728-99

A patriot and a benefactor of the arts who built a casino, the most beautiful edifice in modern Ireland, James Caulfeild was born on 18 August 1728 at Charlemont House, Jervis Street, Dublin, the town house of his parents, James, third Viscount Charlemont, and Elizabeth. One of four children, he lived alternately in Dublin and at Castlecaulfeild on the family lands which, according to tradition, stretched from Slieve Gallion in Co Derry to Slieve Gullion in Co Armagh. Lord Charlemont (he succeeded to the title at the age of six) was considered both shy and delicate and so did not go to school. When his mother died in 1743 he became the ward of Thomas Adderley, who was both his stepfather and a cousin. Charlemont came under the influence of his tutor, Rev Edward Murphy, who, fearful of his young charge's "love of cards and sitting up to late hours," decided to leave Dublin and make a grand tour of Europe. They went by Holland and Germany to Turin, where Charlemont made the acquaintance of the philosopher David Hume in 1748. In Constantinople he visited a mosque, a Turkish bath and, in disguise, the Grand Vizier's levée. Returning by the Greek islands and Athens, Charlemont settled in Rome from 1750-54; there he met Piranesi and William Chambers (later his favoured architect). Charlemont returned home in 1755 but spent much of his time in London where he was a friend of Johnson. But believing that "the Irishman in London, long before he has lost his brogue, loses all Irish ideas," he resolved to live in Ireland. He married Mary Hickman from Co Clare, who gave him five children, and settled at Marino, a country house just to the north of Dublin. There he had built, to Chambers's plan, a casino which stands comparison with Gabriel's Petit-Trianon at Versailles. He also had Chambers design a new townhouse at Rutland (Parnell) Square. Charlemont even had a town plan drawn for the Moy on his Ulster estates on which, though he was seldom in residence, he kept a watchful eye; in 1763 he was made an earl for his damping-down of the Armagh "Oakboy" disturbances. However, he was to make his mark above all as the aristocratic leader of the "Patriot" party, that group of MPs who refused to support the government in return for favours, but instead strove to make Ireland a "nation." It was Charlemont who gave Henry Grattan, the patriot orator, a safe pocket-borough seat in parliament; who became commander-in-chief of the patriotic Volunteers, travelling all over the country to review parades; who welcomed the achievement of parliamentary independence in 1782. But at the Rotunda Volunteer gathering, he used his influence to smother more radical demands for parliamentary reform and Catholic emancipation. Much of his energy was then given to the founding in 1785 of the Royal Irish Academy, of which he was first president. But there was no avoiding politics in a time of revolution: Charlemont lamented the influence of French ideas on Belfast, came to accept the necessity of Catholic emancipation and rejoiced that "we are yet a nation" on the parliamentary defeat of the first attempt to bring about union with Great Britain (January 1799). Before the second, successful attempt, he died in Dublin on 4 August 1799 and was buried at Armagh cathedral.

Susannah Centilivre

?1667-1723

Susannah Centilivre, the actress and playwright, was born almost certainly in 1667 in Co Tyrone, the daughter of a Cromwellian supporter called Freeman who fled his home in Lincoln at the time of the restoration of Charles II. Her mother died when she was twelve and she was so ill-treated by her step-mother that she ran away from home to try her fortunes in England. She was fifteen but tall and very handsome, well fitted to play the "breeches parts" in which she specialised in later years. The accounts of these early days tend to be romantic. One story for which there seems some evidence was that she was befriended by a gentleman called Anthony Hammond with whom she lived in Cambridge for a year. She married twice but both husbands were killed in duels within a year of the weddings. The second husband was named Carroll and it was as Susannah Carroll that she wrote or more probably adapted her first stage success, a tragi-comedy called *The Perjur'd Husband*. She became a strolling player and while acting in Windsor about 1706, playing the part of Alexander the Great, she so impressed Joseph Centilivre, who was chef to Queen Anne and afterwards George I, that he asked her to marry him. Their home at Charing Cross became a meeting place for the literary lions of the day. She became a friend of Steele, Rowe and George Farquhar* and incurred the wrath of Alexander Pope sufficiently to find her place in his blistering satire *The Dunciad*. It is supposed that this was because of her attacks on Catholicism and priests in her plays. She wrote in all nineteen plays between 1700 and 1722, the majority highly successful comedies, and she was generally regarded as a better writer than an actress. Her most famous play was *A Bold Stroke for a Wife* (1718) which contains the character "the real Simon Pure," an expression which was still current proverbially in the early part of the present century. Writing in the *Tatler* her friend Steele said that in her play *The Busy Body* (1709) "the plot and incidents are laid with that subtlety of spirit which is peculiar to females of wit." Her marriage to Centilivre seems to have been happy and made her acquainted with court circles. When she died on 1 December 1723 she left many valuable ornaments which had been presented to her by royalty. She is buried in St Martin's-in-the Fields. Her plaque mentions her Irish origin.

Francis Chesney

1789-1872

Francis Rawdon Chesney, the explorer of the overland route to India, was born at Ballyvea, near Annalong, Co Down on 16 March 1789. He was the son of an Irish emigrant to America, who having fought with Lord Moira and Cornwallis against the insurgent rebels, returned home when the colonists won the War of Independence. The son had early military experience, holding at the age of nine a commission in the yeomanry which was set up to quell the '98 rising. His father's patron, Lord Moira, secured a cadetship for the young man at the military academy at Woolwich and he was stationed at Guernsey during the second war with Napoleon. After Waterloo his free time was spent in the study of tactics. He visited the scenes of Napoleon's principal battlefields and became an expert on military science. He had great personal courage: once he saved the crew of a French barque which had run ashore near his home during a snowstorm by "his intrepidity and powers as a swimmer" as his citation from the *Société des Naufrages* put it. His military career was such that he never saw action in spite of frequently volunteering for active service, so that a mission to explore the Near East was most welcome. Between 1829 and 1832 he travelled in Egypt and Mesopotamia, once with a few Arab companions travelling the length of the Euphrates river by raft. His report on the feasibility of building a canal to the Red Sea from the Mediterranean led de Lesseps to dub him "the father of the Suez canal." Soon after his return he agreed to lead another exploration in that region to try to find a commercial overland route to India. Parliament voted £20,000 for the project though Chesney volunteered to serve without pay. The expedition landed at Antioch (Antakya) in Turkey in 1835 and he transported two small steamboats across the desert to the headwaters of the Euphrates. There one of the vessels was sunk with the loss of twenty lives, but in spite of this and other setbacks he charted the Euphrates, the Tigris and the Karum rivers and completed the passage to India. When he reached England in 1837 the excitement of his return was eclipsed by the death of William IV and the constitutional crisis that preceded the accession of Victoria. In 1843, with the rank of lieut-colonel, he was made commandant of Hong Kong where he remained till 1847. He retired to the family estate of Packolet, near Kilkeel in 1851 but kept his commission, reaching the rank of general in 1868. Chesney continued to make visits to his chosen territory. He was sent to Turkey in 1857 and again in 1863 as chief negotiator for railway concessions and he made a final survey of the Euphrates route. His dream of establishing an overland route to India was frequently postponed because of chronic international dissensions. He died at home on 30 January 1872. Chesney was made a Fellow of the Royal Society and of the Royal Geographical Society and his book *Expedition for the Survey of the Euphrates and the Tigris* (1850) remained a standard work for many years. He also published a manual on firearms and artillery and an account of the Russo-Turkish campaigns of 1828-29. He was probably the most talented soldier who never fought a battle.

Kitty Clive

1711-85

Kitty Clive, the great comic actress, was born Catherine Rafter, probably in Belfast, in 1711. Her father, William Rafter, was a Jacobite lawyer from Kilkenny who found it better economically and politically to practise in London. She joined the company of Colley Cibber during his management of the Theatre Royal, Drury Lane in 1728 and by 1731 was established as one of the leading comic actresses of the day. That year she wed a barrister, George Clive, but the marriage lasted for only a few months. They parted amicably but in the style of theatre programmes of the period she was thereafter known as Mrs Clive. Her forte was low comedy and burlesque of Italian opera. She had a magnificent singing voice and appeared in the first performance of Handel's *Samson.* The composer became one of her friends as did Dr Johnson, Goldsmith, Gay and Horace Walpole. Though her education was scanty these great men of the age sought her company. Johnson once said, "Clive is very good to sit with; she always understands what you say." She was the only actress whose temper the great Garrick feared, but they remained the closest of friends. The cause of dissension was her insistence upon playing unsuitable parts, those in high comedy and tragedy, for which she was unfitted. Her Portia in 1741 opposite Macklin*'s famous Shylock was a disaster. Her voice was dissonant, she moved awkwardly and during the trial scene she gave imitations of leading lawyers and judges of the day. Yet she insisted upon reviving the performance in spite of increasing girth. The most hilarious piece of miscasting was as Desdemona to Macklin's Othello. Kitty Clive retired from the stage on 24 April 1769 and Garrick insisted upon appearing opposite her in her final performance. She retired to a cottage in the grounds of Strawberry Hill, provided by Horace Walpole, and it was christened Clive's Den. There she continued to be hostess to the leading people of the time. Her portrait was painted many times, notably by Hogarth. She died there on 6 December 1785. When she retired Johnson said that "in sprightliness of humour I have never seen her equalled."

John Colgan

c.1582-1658

A contemporary illustration shows him sitting, surrounded by books, uttering the one word, *praeservata*; appropriately, for one who gathered and rewrote accounts of Irish saints for most of his life. John Colgan was born c.1592 at Priestown near Carndonagh, in Inishowen, Co Donegal. After early education in Ireland, he went to one of the Irish colleges in the Netherlands where he was ordained a secular priest in 1618. On 26 April 1620 he took the Franciscan habit at the order's Collège St-Antoine which had been established at Louvain (now Leuven) for the education of Irish friars. Colgan taught philosophy in colleges near Köln and at Mainz before returning to Louvain as master of novices in 1634. A year later, on the death of Aodh Mac an Bháird, Colgan took charge of the Irish Franciscan project to publish an *Acta Sanctorum Hiberniae*. Altogether there would be eight volumes: genealogies of kings, lives of saints, martyrologies, lists of bishops and of priests and churches, and a dictionary. Helped by Bonaventure O'Docharty and other Franciscan friars, Colgan brought out the first volume in 1645: the lives of all Irish saints whose feasts occur in the first three months of the year. The second volume appeared in 1647 and contained lives of Patrick, Brighid and Colum Cille*, collected from manuscripts in places as diverse as Biburg and Aulne-sur-Sambre as well as Ireland. For his knowledge of Irish manuscripts, Colgan depended on Micheál Ó Cleirigh*, an older Franciscan confrère at Louvain; and it was Colgan who gave the name *Annals of the Four Masters* to Ó Cleirigh's great work, *Annála Rioghachta Eireann*. After 1647 Colgan compiled further volumes of the *Acta Sanctorum* but shortage of funds, after Ireland's defeat at the hands of Cromwell, prevented their being published. Besides, Colgan was by now in poor health: in 1650 he refused the position of commissary to the Irish colleges of Louvain, Vielun and Prague, on the grounds that, "on account of old age and continuous scholastic studies, I [am] already very much worn out." Colgan wrote one final short work, on Duns Scotus, before he died at the College of St Anthony, Louvain, on 15 January 1658. His three manuscript volumes, dealing with Irish saints in foreign countries, were lost when the Collège St-Antoine was suppressed at the time of the French revolution. What survived of the work of Colgan and the other Franciscan scholars had to await the interest of a resurgent nationalist Ireland before it was finally published by modern scholars, in the past century.

Colum Cille
521-597

St Colum Cille, who led the mission to christianise
Scotland, a country Ireland had already colonised, was
born a member of the noble Cenél Conaill in what is now
Donegal. This we know from the *Amra*, a eulogy written
c.600. From the *Vita Columbae*, written c.700 by
Adomnán, one of Colum's successors as abbot at Iona,
we can piece together a more detailed biography of the
saint. Born in 521, he was educated in turn with
Cruithnechán, with Gemmán in Leinster and with bishop
Findbarr. Colum's family connection with the Uí Néill
made it difficult for him to remain in Ireland after the
battle of Cúl Drebene, especially if he wished to pursue
the ideals of monasticism, so in 563 he sailed to Scotland
as *peregrinus pro Christo* and established a monastery on
the island of Iona. The island was part of the Gaelic
kingdom of Dál Riata, whose ruler, Áedán mac Gabráin,
Colum had helped bring into political alliance with Áed
mac Ainmerech of the northern Uí Néill, at the royal
conference of Druim Cet. Colum made Iona the
headquarters of a federation of monastic foundations,
both in Ireland (Durrow, Drumhome, perhaps Derry)
and in Scotland (Tiree, Hinba) all of which had Uí Néill
kinsmen as abbots. Close connection with the secular
interests of the Uí Néill made the federation an ideal
system for the survival and continuity of the church in
early Irish society after the saint's death in 597. This
much we know of Colum with reasonable certainty.

Attesting to the folk veneration of the saint, there is a profusion of colourful stories such as the one that he left Ireland to do penance for having copied a bible manuscript without the permission of its owner. In clerical circles too Colum's name was of influence. To support Derry's claim to leadership of the twelfth-century ecclesiastical reform movement, a monk at Derry wrote *Betha Colaim Chille* in which Derry is shown as Colum's first and greatest foundation. To Colum is attributed the poem "Is aire charaimm Doire" with its memorable opening lines:

This is why I love Derry
because of its tranquillity and brightness
for it is full of fair angels
from one end to the other.

Lines not unworthy of Colum who did actually write the "Noli, Pater," with its luminous closing couplet:

Manet in meo corde Dei amoris flamma,
ut in argenti vase auri ponitur gemma.

[The flame of love of God rests in my heart,/ as a gem of gold is placed in a silver vessel]

William Conor

1881-1968

William Conor, the portraitist of Belfast street life, was born on 6 May 1881 in the Old Lodge Road. He attended Clifton Park National School in Avoca Street and later studied at the Government School of Design. He became an apprentice poster designer at David Allen, the company which covered with garish advertisements the many hoardings which were so characteristic of city life. His wages were four shillings and sixpence a week and out of them he was able to save enough to study further at Dublin and Paris. He first exhibited in 1914 and during the war which followed he was appointed by the government to paint official records of soldiers and munition workers. His painting of the "Charge of the Ulster Division at Thiepval" became a postcard for the Ulster Volunteer Force, which had ceased its threat of civil war for the duration of the world conflict. The force ran a hospital instead and used Conor's very popular work to raise money for it. Conor's main interest was in painting the streets of his native city. Shipyard workers, shawlies, children queuing for the pictures, tired people huddled on a jaunting car, the City Hall under snow— these were his favourite subjects, though he painted country scenes as well. He was also in demand as a portrait painter, among his sitters being Douglas Hyde, President of Ireland and Robert Lynd* the Belfast-born essayist. The Second World War saw him again a war artist with subjects like the air raid damage on tram depots and city centre stores, the evacuation of children from Belfast and the coming of the American troops to Northern Ireland. He was a well known figure about the city, clearly an "artist" in a sedate environment. His soft felt hat, large bow tie and silk handkerchief cascading from the breast pocket of a velvet jacket marked him as different. Yet he felt no alienation. He once wrote, "All my life I have been completely absorbed and with affection in the activities of the Belfast people and surrounding country...I trust these paintings and drawings will recall a world that is quickly disappearing and could soon be forgotten." Conor became a member of the Royal Hibernian Academy in 1947, was awarded the OBE in 1952 and was granted a Civil List pension in 1959. He never married but lived in his later years with his sister Mary and surviving brother Russell in a large house in Salisbury Avenue. Mary died in 1958 and a slow domestic deterioration resulted. He died from hypothermia on 6 February 1968. His friend Lynn Doyle* wrote of him,"William Conor has with his art, done more for his native City of Belfast, than has been done for any other city in the United Kingdom; giving permanence in works of masterly draughtsmanship and colouring to Belfast's humbler streets and to a whole generation of workers, by whose hands the glory of Belfast has been exalted."

Henry Cooke

1788-1868

A champion of second-reformation ideology, of orthodox Presbyterianism, of political Protestantism and of unionism, Henry Cooke was born on 11 May 1788 on a tenant farm at Grillagh near Maghera, Co Londonderry, the youngest son of John Cooke (by his second wife, Jane Howie). He was educated locally and then from 1802 at Glasgow College, where he studied arts and divinity. Cooke returned to Glasgow (1815-17) to study metaphysics and elocution and he also studied medicine for a year in Dublin. Cooke's first appointment was as minister to Duneane, near Randalstown, Co Antrim, in 1808. From 1811 he was assistant at Donegore, Co Antrim before being called to Killeleagh, Co Down, as minister in 1818. Finally, in 1829, he was called to the church specially built for him in May Street, Belfast, where he served until the year before his death. It was at Killeleagh that Cooke first publicly championed trinitarianism, against the unitarianism of an itinerant English preacher, John Smethurst (and of the local landlord, Archibald Hamilton Rowan, an old radical). At Presbyterian general synod each year Cooke fought a campaign to purge both church and Belfast Academical Institution of all "arians." Using his great presence, his mastery of oratory and his ability to ridicule, Cooke crushed an able opponent, Henry Montgomery. Step by step he won a complete victory: at Moneymore in 1824 he was elected moderator of general synod; in 1829 he had all members of synod declare their belief in the trinity and so forced the unitarians to secede; in 1840 the general synod and the secession synod united to form the General Assembly of the Presbyterian Church in Ireland. Henry Cooke was also the champion of the cause of Protestantism in general, in Ireland: he argued against Catholic emancipation (in the 1820s), for a national education system influenced by Protestantism (in the 1830s) and against disestablishment of the Church of Ireland (in the 1860s). For Cooke, Protestant political unity was essential to survival, and at a monster-meeting at Hillsborough in 1834 he called for all Protestants to rally to conservatism (in preference to the dangers of liberalism). Naturally for Cooke, conservative meant unionist: "Look at [the prosperity of] Belfast and be a repealer if you can," he declared at an anti-repeal rally in Belfast after Daniel O'Connell's provocative visit in 1841. Cooke lived out his life in the city where his religious and political opinions were so popular. He was so much in demand as a preacher that his May Street congregation complained of how little of him they saw. He became professor (of sacred rhetoric) and then president of the new assembly's Theological College (1846). Warm-hearted and kind in private, Cooke married Ellen Mann of Toome, by whom he had thirteen children. When he died at his residence at the Ormeau Road on 13 December 1868 he was given a public funeral to Balmoral cemetery. Cooke was commemorated by a statue erected in 1875 and known to succeeding generations of Belfast people as "the black man."

James Craig

1871-1940

The humane, unimaginative but competent leader who led Ulster Unionists in their successful attempt to partition Ireland (so as to keep part within the United Kingdom), James Craig was born in north Co Down on 8 January 1871. The seventh child and sixth son of James Craig, the millionaire owner of Dunville's distillery, and of Eleanor (née Gilmore), Craig was educated at a local Presbyterian school and at Merchiston Castle school in Edinburgh. Bored by stockbroking, Craig served in the war against the Boers in South Africa (1900-1). He returned home to a legacy of £100,000 which he used to finance his election as MP for East Down in 1903. He married Cecil Mary Tupper, an Englishwoman who gave him both a family of three children and constant support in his political life. At the time Craig went into politics, Protestant Ulster was unionist, almost to a man. Craig organised a demonstration of 50,000 at his home, Craigavon, on 25 September 1911 to show how serious Ulster was in its opposition to Home Rule for Ireland, and this persuaded Carson* to lead the Unionists. Craig organised the signing of the Ulster Covenant by half a million people in 1912, encouraged the organisation of the Ulster Volunteer Force and supported the running of 35,000 rifles from Germany (1914). Unlike Carson, Presbyterian Craig had no philosophical qualms about organising rebellion. By 1914, the British government had been forced to accept that unionist Ulster must be treated differently from the rest of Ireland. Craig ensured that the UVF formed the nucleus of a special 36th (Ulster) division in the 1914-18 war and he was the quartermaster-general. But he was not well enough for active service and returned to politics where he became a baronet (1917) and acting First Lord of the Admiralty in 1920. In government Craig used his influence to ensure that Northern Ireland was established as a six (rather than nine) county unit and that the power of the senate to represent minority views was reduced. The creation of Northern Ireland was Craig's greatest achievement and it was natural that he should become Prime Minister there. He had a 14,000 majority (over de Valera) for Co Down in the 1921 election, and from then until his death he was returned unopposed to the Northern parliament. As Prime Minister, Craig channelled most loyalist aggression into the discipline of the special constabulary, he defeated the IRA campaign of the 1920s and he won a measure of respect from Cosgrave's government in the Free State. Unfortunately for Northern Ireland, his failures were greater. In his negotiations on financial matters with the Westminster government (which he conducted from his second home at Cleeve Court on the Thames) he failed to make Northern Ireland's case forcibly enough. He had no policy to deal with the province's economic problems of declining industry and massive unemployment. Above all, though amiable with individual Catholics like Joe Devlin*, he allowed himself to be influenced by his more uncompromising supporters in his treatment of the Catholic minority. He put the unsuitable Dawson Bates in charge of home affairs, he failed to take account of Catholic susceptibilities about education, he abolished PR as an electoral system, he permitted the gerry-mandering of local government boundaries in

Londonderry and he allowed discrimination which kept Catholic representation in the upper civil service at six per cent and in the RUC at seventeen per cent. Craig's last years were dogged by ill-health which he tried to ameliorate by long sea-cruises. By 1938 he was so unwell that even admirers like Spender, the cabinet secretary, thought he should resign. But Craig loved the glory of his position (he became a viscount in 1927) and felt he could not do without the salary. He died in office on 24 November 1940, mourned by Unionists as a hero. For later historians he was the only man who just might have saved Ulster unionists from themselves but who showed himself too weak for the job.

Francis Crozier

1796-1848

Captain Francis Rawdon Moira Crozier, the polar explorer, was born in Banbridge, Co Down in September 1796. He joined the British navy as a boy sailor in 1810 and sailed on the *Hamadryad*, seeing service in the Pacific and South Atlantic. He became a midshipman (that first step towards becoming an officer) in June 1812. He had early experience of polar voyage and exploration, first accompanying Captain Parry on the Arctic journey of the *Hecla* when he was twenty-five. By 1827, now commissioned as a lieutenant, he had been in Arctic waters on three trips and had become known as a kind of polar expert. He was sent to Baffin Bay and the Davis Strait on the west coast of Greenland in search of missing whalers and on his return in the year 1837 was promoted to the rank of commander. He was master of the *Terror*, one of the ships that accompanied Ross on his Antarctic expedition. His last great journey was as part of the ill-fated Franklin expedition to find a north-west passage between Canada, Greenland and Russia. The expedition left on 26 May 1845 with Franklin in command of the *Erebus* and Crozier, now captain, on the *Terror*. They were last seen on 26 July in Baffin Bay making good progress, but after that there was no further word. By the autumn of 1847 anxiety was beginning to be expressed. No fewer than twenty expeditions were dispatched to try to find them. In 1854 a Dr Rae learned from Eskimos that in 1850 forty men were seen dragging a boat over the ice north of King William Island. The last expedition fitted out by Lady Franklin, Sir John's widow, left on 30 June 1857 under the command of Captain Francis McClintock in the yacht *Fox*. In 1859 one of his sledge parties discovered a handwritten record describing the final fate of the expedition. They had discovered the North-West Passage that was the point of the expedition but had been held by pack-ice during the year 1846. Franklin died on 11 June 1847 and Crozier took command. By this date the expedition had lost twenty-four men and he decided to make his way back. It was presumed that he and the remainder of the party died of hunger and scurvy, though two unidentifiable skeletons were the only remains ever discovered. McClintock, himself an Irishman (from Dundalk) named the western promontory of King William Island Cape Crozier and reckoned that Crozier's death had taken place some time in 1848. The expedition remained a source of much speculation throughout the 19th century. Much was written about the possible fate of the explorers and stories of white men discovered living among eskimos were rife.

Joe Devlin
1871-1934

The leading Northern nationalist politician both before and after the partition settlement of 1921, Joseph Devlin was born on 13 February 1871 at Hamill Street, Belfast. He was the fourth son of Charles and Elizabeth (née King) who had migrated from the Loughshore area of Tyrone to Belfast. Educated at Christian Brothers School, Divis Street, Devlin worked in a public-house before becoming a journalist, at first with the *Irish News* and then as Belfast correspondent of the *Freeman's Journal*. A talented debater, he showed an interest in politics as early as 1886 when he helped Thomas Sexton win West Belfast for the nationalists. Devlin became secretary of the Belfast Young Ireland Society and then took up a post at party headquarters in Dublin. Afterwards he became secretary of the United Irish League and made a number of visits to the USA to liaise with Irish-American nationalists. His career as a public representative began in 1902 when he was unopposed at a bye-election in North Kilkenny. In 1906 he regained West Belfast for the Irish Party and held the seat until 1918. One reason for Devlin's success was his refounding of the Ancient Order of Hibernians as a political machine to rival that of the Orange Order. In 1913 he helped organise the Irish National Volunteers but had no sympathy for the minority who used armed force in 1916. In 1918 that minority became the Sinn Féin majority over the Irish Party, the leadership of which Devlin had astutely refused on the death of John Redmond. Instead Devlin stayed close to his own grass-roots and held Falls against de Valera himself in 1918. Devlin was a member of the new Northern Ireland parliament from 1921 until his death, at first for West Belfast and then for Belfast Central. He was also an MP for Fermanagh and Tyrone at Westminster from 1929. At Stormont, Devlin and the nationalists pursued a policy of "creeping abstentionism" but attended parliament when they felt vital Catholic interests were involved. Devlin defended Catholic education as a right; fought unsuccessfully for the retention of proportional representation (on the grounds that it enfranchised Catholic minorities, as in North Antrim); campaigned for a comprehensive public housing scheme in order to abolish slums; and, as a director of a Belfast bakery, opposed the wheat quota bill of 1932. Small, thick-set, black-haired, Devlin was immensely popular with his constituents and received an average of thirty letters a day. When he died, unmarried, in Belfast on 18 February 1934, "Wee Joe" was mourned by people all over Ireland, and even though he had used his great oratorical gifts to castigate them, unionist government representatives joined all other Irish political parties to follow his coffin.

John Doherty

c.1798-1854

A trade-union organiser and radical journalist in Britain, John Doherty was born in Buncrana, Co Donegal, probably in 1798. Little is known about his background save that it was poor and therefore undocumented. From the age of ten he worked at a textile mill in his native town. As a youth he moved to Larne to work as a cotton-spinner and then, in 1816, emigrated to Manchester where wages were higher. There he was a leading figure in the Manchester spinners union for nearly twenty years. While working in George Murray's New Mill, Doherty was involved in the spinners' strike of 1818, to the extent that he was afterwards imprisoned. In 1824-5 he attempted to form a federal union of spinners from all areas and he opposed the re-enactment by parliament of the combination laws, which sought to outlaw trade union activity. In 1829 he led the spinners of Manchester in a six-month strike against wage reductions. In the same year he initiated the Grand General Union of Operative Cotton Spinners throughout the United Kingdom. Within a year this early attempt at a consolidated union had failed, as did Doherty's National Association for the Protection of Labour. But they were to provide an example for Robert Owen, whom Doherty supported, and for other more successful union organisers later on. In 1832 Doherty set up a bookshop, printing business and radical reading-rooms at Withy Grove in Manchester. From there he edited and published his best-known journal, *The Voice of the People*. He declared that his aim was "to better the condition of the people—to have them stand erect and look boldly in the faces of their masters, and to tell them, 'We are not your slaves, we are your equals.'" Every radical cause met with his support, from planning a national convention to force parliament to grant household suffrage in 1832, to attempting to secure radical control of Manchester local government. He was involved in the cooperative and the temperance movements and in the fight for working-class education. An Irish nationalist and a devout Catholic, he encouraged the Ashton-Stalybridge strikers to be "as united as the Catholics of Ireland [and] you will be blessed with similar success." That he was a number of times in jail for libel was a tribute to the undiluted radicalism of his writing. But it did not make life easy for his English wife, who reared their five children and helped run the bookshop. Nor can it have helped that Doherty was fiery-tempered and inconsistent. But his weaknesses were outweighed by his generosity, his organising ability, his eloquence and his resilience in the face of defeat. Deteriorating health forced him to retire from public life in the late 1840s, and when he died on 14 April 1854 he was a forgotten man who received the briefest of obituaries in the *Manchester Guardian*. However, his importance in the history of British trade unionism was recognised in a biography by Kirby and Musson published in 1975.

Lynn Doyle

1873-1961

Lynn Doyle, the humorist and playwright, was born Leslie Alexander Montgomery on 5 October 1873 in Downpatrick, Co Down. He was educated in Dundalk and became a clerk with the Northern Bank in Belfast in 1898. He was part of the Ulster Literary Theatre movement which was founded by Bulmer Hobson* and David Parkhill in 1902 and wrote *Love and Land* (1913), *The Summons* (1918), *The Lilac Ribbon* (1919) and *The Turncoats* (1922) for the the theatreless company. Pseudonyms were common at the time: Sam Waddell called himself "Rutherford Mayne," Harry Morrow signed himself "Gerald MacNamara," Charles Kerr preferred "C K Ayre" and for a bank clerk with an extremely conservative company some formal disguise was appropriate when associating with "playactors." While trying to think of a suitable pseudonym, Montgomery saw one day a large tin of linseed oil in a paint shop and for a while his work was signed "Lynn C Doyle." After some time when he began to write his humorous books he dropped the "C." The first of his funny books, *Ballygullion,* was published in 1908 and the last, *The Ballygullion Bus,* in 1957. He wrote twenty books in all, about a dozen of them set in the northern village of Ballygullion which takes its name from a part of his native Downpatrick. They are full of pawky but uncondescending Ulster humour and deal gently with northern sectarianism. The character of Patrick Murphy, the philosophical Catholic small tenant farmer, is better than any equivalent in Somerville and Ross and Mr Anthony, the fussy and accident-prone small-town solicitor, is a richly comic creation. The stories remain very funny and give a reasonably accurate picture of life in East Ulster before the present bitterness. Doyle continued to compose after he retired from the banking service. He wrote a number of straight novels and many serious short stories which showed a considerable talent and a grasp of the realities of Irish history. He lived in Dublin and was one of the first writers to be appointed to the Censorship of Publications Board in 1937 but he resigned quite soon afterwards. He was in much demand as a lecturer in his later years and wrote a charming chapter of autobiography, *An Ulster Childhood* , in 1954. He died in Dublin on 18 August 1961.

Saumarez Dubourdieu

1717-1812

The last Huguenot clergyman in Lisburn to conduct services in French, Saumarez Dubourdieu was born in 1717 in London, the son of Jean-Armand Dubourdieu and Charlotte Massey. Saumarez Dubourdieu's father was among the 200,000 Huguenots or French Protestants who, rather than see their churches closed, their clergy banished and their children reared as Catholics, fled France on the revocation of the Edict of Nantes in 1685. After the early death of his father, Dubourdieu *fils* was reared in Dublin where he studied at Trinity College. Though the Huguenots were Calvinist and found Anglicanism "très opposé à la simplicité de notre réformation," those who came to Ireland nearly all conformed to the Church of Ireland, of which Dubourdieu became a minister. At first Dubourdieu founded a school at Hillsborough, Co Down, where he married Mary, the daughter of Rev Shem Thompson. But then he moved to Lisburn, Co Antrim, where a sizeable proportion of the 10,000 Huguenot refugees who had come to Ireland were involved in the linen business. Dubourdieu's family were no strangers to Lisburn; in 1689 his great-uncle Jean had been there as a chaplain to the Duke of Schomberg who was preparing for the battle of the Boyne, and, until his death in 1756, another great-uncle, Charles de la Valade, had been minister of the French Church in Castle Street. In 1756 Saumarez Dubourdieu started a classical school in Bow Street, Lisburn, and continued his great-uncle's ministry to the Huguenot community. In the French Church each Sunday, he read from the Book of Common Prayer (in French translation) but for the psalms he used the favourite version of the Huguenots, the *Pseaumes de David mis en rime Françoise par Clement Marot et Theodore de Bèze*. Dubourdieu ministered to the Huguenot community (with names like Crommelin, De La Cherois, Gillot and Roché) for over fifty years, but already in 1780, when he had become rector of the parish (of Glenavy), a new generation was becoming bilingual and the French language services were falling into abeyance. Dubourdieu died on 14 December 1812, leaving two daughters and three sons (one of whom, John, became rector of Annahilt and wrote a *Statistical Survey of the County of Down* in 1802). But even if younger Huguenots became hibernicised, Saumarez Dubourdieu remained a Frenchman; as the commemorative tablet in Lisburn Cathedral had it; "Descended from French parentage, exiled from his homeland, he earned for himself by his virtues, a name, a habitation, and a new homeland among strangers."

Charles Gavan Duffy

1816-1903

Charles Gavan Duffy, the nationalist journalist and politician, was born in Monaghan on Good Friday, 12 April 1816, the son of a prosperous local shopkeeper who also had a share in a bleach green. He was almost entirely self-educated and began a long career of journalism with work in Belfast and Dublin on the *Morning Register*. It was he who gave Fr Mathew, the temperance preacher, the idea of setting up reading-rooms to give the urban poor an alternative to the public house as a means of entertainment. A meeting with Thomas Davis and Davis's friend John Blake Dillon led to the formulation, "under a noble elm," of the idea for a weekly journal that would begin the re-acculturation that the Young Ireland movement insisted must accompany any resurgence of cultural nationalism. The *Nation*'s first edition went on sale on 8 October 1842 and though it sold at the expensive price of sixpence, it soon had a wider circulation than any other newspaper in Ireland. Duffy, the only one of the three with journalistic experience, was editor, though in fact most of the editorial writing was done by Davis. Davis's tragically early death a month before his thirty-first birthday in 1845 and the three years of famine that followed delayed any overt action that the paper's militancy seemed to prescribe. Then in 1848 when revolution was in the air Duffy was arrested and held in Newgate, "under vile conditions" which permanently affected his health. He was released after an abortive and ill-planned rising by Smith O'Brien and Thomas Meagher, and in the company of Thomas Carlyle toured the country which had been ravaged by hunger, disease and emigration. He threw himself into agitation again, revived and improved the *Nation* and in 1852 was elected MP for New Ross. Frustration, inevitable in the parliament of the time, and what he considered undue clerical influence in Irish politics made Duffy lose heart. He had become something of an expert on the new colony of Australia through serving on a Commons select committee and it seemed that here was a place where his talents would be appreciated. He sold the *Nation* and emigrated to Victoria to practise law. (He had been called to the Irish bar after study in King's Inns in 1845 but had never practised.) His last editorial for his paper contained the famous peroration: "...there seems no more hope for the Irish cause than for the corpse on the dissecting-table." His career down under prospered. He entered the state legislature of Victoria, became prime minister in 1871 and accepted a knighthood for services to the colony in 1873. It was as Sir Charles Gavan Duffy that he retired to France in 1880. Before his death in 1903 he completed a life of Davis, a history of the Young Ireland movement and an autobiography, *My Life in Two Hemispheres*. He died on 9 February 1903.

Johannes Duns Scotus

c.1266-1308

Johannes (or John) Duns Scotus, scholastic philosopher and theologian, was born in 1265 or 1266, in Co Down, according to his biographer and editor Luke Wadding, though his birthplace has been the subject of much discussion. He entered the Franciscan order and studied at Merton College, Oxford. He succeeded to the chair of divinity there in 1301, his tenure becoming the inspiration for one of Gerald Manley Hopkins's most famous sonnets. He was proposed by the head of the order as lecturer at Paris, then the centre of learning, and in 1307, a year before his death, he taught at Cologne. He died there on 8 November 1308. His writings are voluminous and, edited in twelve volumes by Wadding, deal with grammar and science but are mainly concerned with philosophy and theology. Like his rival Thomas Aquinas he was interested in Aristotle but his principal theological work is the *Opus Oxoniense*, a commentary upon Peter Lombardi's *Sentences*. True to Franciscan tradition he followed Augustine and was critical of Aquinas. He rejected the contention of the rationalists that philosophy was sufficient to satisfy man's desire for an understanding of his own nature because even so profound a philosopher as Aristotle must be ignorant of the fall and man's need for grace and redemption. In theology Duns Scotus strongly upheld the doctrine of the Immaculate Conception. He insisted further on the necessity for revelation: man could not attain to an absolute knowledge of God by reason alone. In philosophy he revived nominalism though in a milder form and denied the real distinction between essence and existence. He stressed the contingent nature of the universe and its total dependence upon God's creative will. Duns Scotus also followed the traditional Franciscan elevation of the will above the intellect. For his work upon the doctrine of universals he was given the title "Doctor Subtilis." He was essentially a reconciler of tradition with contemporary thought, incorporating only those aspects of Aristotelianism which were compatible with Augustine's intuitions. With the coming of the new thought in the sixteenth century his followers were pilloried as opponents of learning, and "dunces" came to mean those slow or incapable of learning. He was buried in Cologne with the epitaph:

Scotia me genuit, Anglia me suscepit,
Gallia me docuit, Colonia me tenet.
[Ireland bore me, England received me
France taught me, Cologne holds me]

St John Ervine

1883-1971

St John Ervine, the dramatist, novelist, biographer and critic, was born on 28 December 1883 in Ballymacarret, a working-class district of East Belfast. His given name was John Greer Ervine, the Greer being his mother's maiden name. Both his parents were deaf mutes and the main influence in the boy's life was his maternal grandmother who had a shop in the Albertbridge Road. His experience there gave his plays and novels about such small businesses their authenticity. He began working in an insurance office when he was fourteen and three years later transferred to similar work in London. With his background and enthusiasm for Shaw he inevitably became a member of the Fabian Society, but really a rather conservative one. His wife, Leonora Mary Davis, whom he married in 1911 was also a member and well to the right of the movement. He met Yeats and so impressed him by his talent and industry that his first full-length play, *Mixed Marriage*, was produced at the Abbey in the year of his marriage and he became manager of the theatre in 1915. His tenure was brief and stormy (though he did find time to direct *John Ferguson*, one of his strongest plays, in October 1915) and was not helped by the recrudescence in him of a native unionism at the outbreak of the Easter Rising. He turned against all things nationalist, referred to all the Irish who were not authenticated unionists as "Eireanns" and was left by the end of 1916 without any actors, having sacked the few who had not already resigned. To Yeats's and Lady Gregory's relief he asked to be relieved from his post and joined the Dublin Fusiliers to fight in World War I. He was severely wounded in action in France and had to have a leg amputated. While he was with the Abbey he proposed to run it as an ordinary repertory theatre and considered that Irish dramatic writing was of a very low standard. He moved to England and settled, like Sean O'Casey, in Devon. He worked as a drama critic for the *Morning Post* and the *Observer* and became the kind of playwright whose plays he would have liked to stage at the Abbey. During the 1920s he wrote very successful drawing-room comedies and in the Thirties returned to Ulster themes. *Boyd's Shop*, by far his most popular Irish play, was written for the The Play-House in Liverpool in 1936 and had Michael Redgrave and Rachel Kempson in its first production. It opened in the Abbey shortly afterwards. His other popular Ulster play, *Friends and Relations,* was produced in the Abbey in 1941. Ervine was a complete man of letters. Two significant novels about Belfast life (or rather the need to escape from Belfast life) *The Foolish Lovers* (1920) and *The Wayward Man* (1927) showed a grasp of realism that was comparable to Bennett or Galsworthy. Yet his rejection of all things Irish that were not northern and unionist debilitated him as an artist and his five other novels are unmemorable. His biographies, though competently written, showed the same bias. His books on Carson*(1915) and Craig*(1949) were uncritical not to say adulatory, while his appraisal of Oscar Wilde (1951) showed a lack of sympathy with the subject unique among biographers. He was on firmer ground with General Booth, the founder of the Salvation Army, in *God's Soldier* (1935) and his massive life of Bernard Shaw (1956) was a work of genuine devotion and hero-worship. Ervine continued to be the visible and vocal defender of the Northern Ireland state and could scarcely bring himself to be civil about the rest of the country. Yet Robert Lynd*, a near contemporary and a man of diametrically opposite views, still found him very charming. It seems that by rejecting Ireland rather than retaining spiritual nationality and the right to criticise he lost his artistic base, and when he died on 24 January 1971 he was remembered more for his polemical journalism and his Ulster comedies than for any lasting contribution to literature.

George Farquhar

1677-1707

George Farquhar, the last and much the most decorous of the Restoration dramatists, was born in Derry in 1677, the son of the Rev John Farquhar, the prebendary of Raphoe, a small town fifteen miles away. It is likely that his mother was in Derry for the birth because of superior hospital facilities in the city. He attended the Free School and was either sent home during the city's Jacobite siege (1688-89) or braved the hardships. There is a tradition that he was at the Battle of the Boyne. Certainly his first published work, written in 1691 when he was fourteen, was a "Pindarick on the Death of General Schomberg kill'd at the Boyne." He went to Trinity as a sizar, the records showing the enrolment on 17 July 1674 of "Georgius Farquhar, Sizator." He was a diligent student and won an exhibition worth £4 which was, however, taken away because of his involvement in an "affray at Donnybrook Fair" and atheism. The latter charge originated in his comment upon Christ's walking on the water, that the Man born to be hanged need not fear drowning. His exhibition was returned but soon afterwards he left Trinity and was employed as a proofreader at his brother Peyton's printing works and as an actor in the theatre in Smock Alley. He gave up acting in 1697 after nearly killing a fellow actor when he carelessly forgot to exchange his sword for a stage foil. The manager of Smock Alley, Robert Wilks, arranged for a benefit and later followed Farquhar to London to become the main actor in his plays. Farquhar led the life of the intermittently successful playwright, finding mistresses among the complaisant actresses of Drury Lane. Venereal disease was a constant risk, as the text of Farquhar's plays makes clear, but his greater fear was that his tuberculosis would develop. By the end of the troubled century Farquhar was an established playwright with such successes as *Love and a Bottle* (1698), *The Constant Couple* (1699) and *Sir Harry Wildair* (1701). In 1700 he was in the Low Countries as a kind of accepted camp-follower in William III's campaigns and he was commissioned later in the Grenadier Guards, the post being procured for him by Charles Boyle, Earl of Orrery. He was sent to Lichfield as recruiting officer, an experience which gave him material for his popular play *The Recruiting Sergeant* (1706). For all his popularity he never made much money from his comedies. Then in 1703 he met Margaret Pernell, the widow of an army officer who was ten years his senior. He married her thinking that she had expectations but was sorely disappointed. All she brought to the marriage were three children by her former husband. Farquhar took the disappointment well and she bore him two daughters. By 1705 he was definitely ill with pulmonary tuberculosis but he worked steadily at his last and best play, *The Beaux' Stratagem*. He died on 29 April 1707 even as it was being presented successfully in the Theatre Royal. This last play and *The Recruiting Sergeant* are part of the repertory of the British classical theatre and are constantly revived. They are sunny and witty but still suggest, especially in their concern for women, the vicious and dangerous nature of the London society of the period.

Brian Faulkner

1921-77

The unionist pragmatist, who progressed from leading
provocative Orange parades to a belief in power-sharing
and an "Irish dimension," was christened Arthur Brian
Deane at Helen's Bay, Co Down (18 February 1921). He
was the son of James Faulkner, who made his fortune
manufacturing the famous "Faulat" shirt. Though
Presbyterian, Faulkner was educated at St Columba's, a
predominantly Church of Ireland school in Dublin
(1935-9). This helped him mix easily in the South, as did
family holidays in Achill, a love of horses and unfailing
attendance at the Dublin horse show. Faulkner broke off
his law studies at QUB to enter the family business where
he remained from 1940-60. His joining the Orange order
(1946) and involvement in the provocative Longstone
Road march (1955) gave him an anti-Catholic image.
Orange order membership was of course essential to
ensure his becoming a unionist MP at Stormont (for East
Down in 1949). A practical administrative talent allowed
him become Chief Whip (1956) and three years later take
charge of home affairs (where he failed to redress inequity
in the local government franchise, but did make some
reforms in the penal system). But he was happiest as the
Minister of Commerce (1963-9) who brought new
industries (Ford, Michelin) to Ulster in the prosperous
1960s. Faulkner resented O'Neill's victory in the contest
to replace Brookeborough as prime-minister, and though
he saw the need for O'Neill's policy of better relations

with Catholics and with the South, he resigned (January 1969) in protest against O'Neill's "remoteness and indecision." After O'Neill's defeat, Faulkner came back as Minister of Development (May 1969), and at last became Premier (March 1971). His offer of a committee system in parliament was too late to defuse street violence resulting from civil rights marches; his introduction of internment was disastrous, showing he had neither intelligence of the IRA nor understanding of the Catholic community. After the imposition of direct rule (22 March 1972), Faulkner vented his anger, then went on a long holiday, and returned converted to power-sharing and the "Irish dimension." He accepted an institutional relationship with the Republic (at Sunningdale, December 1973), and became Chief Minister of the Northern Ireland executive, a coalition of all Northern political parties (1 January 1974). Forced to resign by the Ulster Workers' Council strike (May 1974) Faulkner formed the Unionist Party of Northern Ireland to defend his ideas, but left politics soon afterwards (1976) to become Baron Faulkner of Downpatrick. In 1951 he married Lucy Forsythe, whom he met at the Iveagh hunt. It was while riding with the same hunt that he fell from his mount and was killed (3 March 1977).

Harry Ferguson

1884-1960

Harry Ferguson, the inventor and pioneer of agricultural machinery, was born Henry George at the family farm at Growell near Hillsborough in Co Down on 4 November 1884. His father was a member of the Plymouth Brethren and the young Ferguson, finding home life narrow and stifling and farming work laborious, became a mechanic in Belfast when he was sixteen. Here he showed a particular aptitude for tuning engines, and an inventive skill that led to modifications in the primitive motor-cycles of the day which he raced without apparent thought for his safety. He also built and flew the first Irish aeroplane. The "mad mechanic", as he was known, took off into force nine winds on the 31 December 1909 and flew for a creditable 130 yards. It was the first aircraft to have a tricycle undercarriage—a device which became common in the design of passenger aeroplanes fifty years later. He gave up flying at the request of his wife, Maureen, whom he married in 1913. He was a strong supporter of the Ulster Volunteer Force and was active in the gun-running that was to arm the force before the First World War. During the war he was asked by the government to devise machinery which would help the "Grow More Food" campaign and, remembering the clumsy mechanised ploughs that had to be dragged between two steam engines placed at different ends of the field, decided to invent a plough which would be mounted on a tractor. This was the first step in designing his own tractor with the mounted implements hydraulically controlled. The prototype was built in Belfast in 1935 and in 1939 he joined forces with Henry Ford in a famous "handshake" agreement to market the Fordson tractor. Between 1940 and 1947, in spite of the war and steel rationing, the company sold 306,000 tractors and nearly a million associated implements. In 1947, after the deaths of Henry Ford and his son Edsel, the owner of the company, Henry Ford II, repudiated the unwritten contract. Ferguson's earnings dropped from $59 million in the first six months to $11 million in the second half of that year. Ferguson responded character-istically: he built his own factory in Detroit near to Ford's major plant and recorded sales of $33 million a year by 1949. He also filed a suit against Ford which resulted in a prolonged piece of litigation and a final award to Ferguson in 1952 of $9.25 million. After this his inventive genius was devoted to the car and in particular to ideas for automatic transmission and a device for preventing the locking of wheels during a skid. He died suddenly on 25 October 1960 at his home in Stow-in-the-Wold in the Cotswolds. He remained a man of great independence of mind and action, a talented loner who was perhaps impatient with the lazy and the easygoing. He refused a knighthood for inventive services to the Allies during the Second World War and always insisted that the battle with Ford was not for money but for the rights of the small inventor against the big corporations.

Sir Samuel Ferguson

1810-86

North of the M2 motorway in Co Antrim, between exits 6 and 5, the east-bound passenger in the fast-driven car may notice on his left a high earthwork called the Dunagore Moat and beside it a rather attractive little church. In the churchyard lie the remains of one who should more appropriately have been interred in St Patrick's Cathedral in Dublin. It was here in Co Antrim that the ancestors of Samuel Ferguson owned land and to here that he often in imagination returned; and here he was buried at his own command. He was born in Belfast in 1810 and educated at the Royal Belfast Academical Institution and later at Trinity which he left without taking a degree. He began writing poems early: "The Forging of the Anchor," composed when he was twenty-one, was one of few poems written about the Belfast shipyard, and when he was studying law at Lincoln's Inns his ballad "Anna Grace" recalled for him the trim beauties of the Ulster countryside. The rest of his life was spent in Dublin where he became friendly with Petrie, O'Donovan and O'Curry and was part of a national revival that foundered as so much else with the great hunger of the 1840s. He admired Thomas Davis and wrote one of his best poems as a lament for the lost leader of Young Ireland. His nationalistic fervour, inspired by the discovery of an ancient literature and the charisma of the founders of *The Nation,* reached its high point in his successful defence of Richard Dalton Williams, himself a poet, who was arraigned for his part in the Smith O'Brien insurrection of 1848. Thereafter his liberal unionism reasserted itself; he married Mary Guinness, a member of a lateral branch of the famous family, and gradually was subsumed into Ascendancy Ireland. He retired from the Irish Bar in 1867, became Deputy Keeper of Public Records and in 1878 was knighted for his work in the organisation of the department, of which he later became president. He had written much on Irish antiquities for the Royal Irish Academy and was to use the bardic material to write epic poetry. In this genuine interest in Irish material he was one of the forerunners of the Yeatsian literary renaissance and deserves his place beside Mangan and Davis in the poem in which Yeats accounted himself brother of those who sang to sweeten Ireland's wrong. His own poetry, including translations from the Irish, is still frequently anthologised. His house in North Great George's Street was a meeting-place for all who valued art and literature. His last months were spent in a friend's cottage in Howth writing dramatic monologues in the style of Browning on the subject of the Phoenix Park murders. He died in Howth on 9 August 1886.

Alec Foster

1890-1972

The greatest three-quarter ever to grace Ulster rugby, Alexander R Foster was born in June 1890 at 39 William Street, Derry, the son of a relieving-officer father and a mother who was caretaker of the local dispensary. At Foyle College, he was an all-round sportsman, playing both rugby and cricket as well as being an oarsman and a swimmer. His rugby career began in earnest in 1908 when he went to Queen's University, Belfast. Here he captained the college team until 1912. He was immediately chosen for the Ulster provincial team, of which he was captain ten times in all. First capped for Ireland in 1910, when he played in the matches against France, England and Scotland, he went on to win eleven caps before the outbreak of war in 1914 and three others when the rugby internationals were resumed at the end of the war. Foster captained the national team six times and was a team selector for three seasons (1922-4). Perhaps his greatest rugby-playing achievement was to play in two test matches of the British and Irish tour of South Africa in 1910. Of course, as well as being a great sportsman, Alec Foster was an able scholar, taking a first in classics at QUB. In 1913, the year after he graduated, he worked in London but then returned to Derry to teach at Foyle College and play rugby for City of Derry. After the war ended he taught for a year at Glasgow High School before returning to Belfast in 1921, first to teach at "Inst" and then to go to Belfast Royal Academy as headmaster in 1923. In 1943 he resigned and went to live near Dublin. By then his first marriage to Anne, sister of Robert Lynd*, had failed and after her death in 1945, Foster married Betty Guidera. In all Foster had four children, one of whom, Christine, married the historian and politician, Conor Cruise O'Brien. In 1965 Alec Foster returned to Belfast where he did some part-time teaching and became involved in radical politics. He was a member of the Wolfe Tone Society and helped draw up the constitution of the Northern Ireland Civil Rights Association. He protested vehemently against allowing the Springboks rugby team to tour Ireland while apartheid was still in force in South Africa. Foster died on 24 August 1972 in hospital in Bantry, Co Cork; up to a month before he had been deeply involved in a campaign to keep open Magee University College in his native city.

Vere Foster

1819-1900

The great benefactor of emigrants, of the national school system and of the Irish National Teachers Organisation was twenty-eight years old when he first visited Ireland. For though he was a Co Louth Foster, Vere Henry Louis was born at Copenhagen (26 April 1819) where his father, Augustus, the British ambassador, and his mother Albinia (née Hobart, a niece of the Earl of Buckinghamshire) resided. He later lived in Turin (1824-38) and was sent to Eton and Oxford where he was undistinguished academically. Afterwards Foster served as a diplomat at Rio de Janeiro and Montevideo (1846-7). There he ceased to be a Christian and, returning to an Ireland which had been stricken by famine (1845-7), he found himself imbued with a mission somehow to aid this country of his Anglo-Irish forebears. He set up a fund to help emigrants, to which he subscribed £10,000 of his own money. He himself made a trip to America as an emigrant on board the *Washington* (1850) and his report of the awful conditions led to the setting-up of a parliamentary select committee at Westminster which laid down minimum standards for emigrant ships. Foster spent a year in the USA, travelling 10,500 miles, studying how emigrants fared, and meeting everyone of importance (including Father Mathew, whose temperance crusade he praised). Later, when the pressure to emigrate had eased, Foster turned his attention to the education system. Believing in the national school ideal of integrating the education of Catholic and Protestant children, he offered to help fund the building of primary schools in Co Louth. But as all the churches and especially the Catholics, opposed the idea, Foster instead used his money to supply poor western schools with essential materials. He disbursed large amounts of money and was involved in correspondence with innumerable grateful teachers and clerical managers. A move to live in Belfast (1867) may have been a result of Foster's friendship with John Ward of Marcus Ward and Co, the publishers. It was this firm which was to produce the "Vere Foster's Copy Books" used in all Irish primary schools to encourage well-rounded handwriting. The venture was a success and the profits were distributed to the poorer schools. Foster was so well known to teachers that he was asked to be the first president of the Irish National Teachers Association, founded in 1868, and which was later to become the INTO. Litigation with Marcus Ward & Co, and disagreements with Parnellite nationalists about his scheme to help young women to emigrate, clouded Foster's declining years. But he continued his own headstrong way, travelling again to America, warning the British government about Irish republican political feeling there, collecting for emigrants and schools and the Royal Belfast Hospital, and as always disbursing his own money. When he died on 21 December 1900 in Belfast, having refused the comfort of his nephew's house at Glyde Court, near Ardee, Foster was in a state of near penury. The house where he died, 115 Great Victoria Street, is marked with a memorial plaque placed there by the INTO, the great teachers' union Foster helped consolidate.

Patrick Gallagher

1873-1964

"Paddy the Cope" was born at Cleendra, near Dungloe on Christmas Day 1871, the eldest son of a family of nine who lived on a poor holding of reclaimed bogland. The Rosses, as the region is known, is an area of comparative prosperity nowadays, but it was a poor rocky barren place at the time of his birth. As Æ* who played a significant part in The Cope's work, wrote in 1916, "If the traveller visits the district he wonders how men ever came to settle there, what necessity drove them to make their homes in a region where the rocky ribs of earth break everywhere through its skin." The land was poor, the tenant farmers had many mouths to feed and most of them were born in debt to the local traders who were called "gombeen" men from the Irish word *gaimbín*, meaning literally "an extra piece" and used to signify "interest." The debts to these traders were never paid off and the money earned from hiring out children to work in the prosperous farms of the Laggan valley in Derry, Tyrone and East Donegal and further cash hard won on farms and from labouring work in Scotland went mainly to reduce this crushing debt. Other pittances were earned by the womenfolk knitting gloves and stockings. The Cope's life followed this pattern; at the age of ten he was hired out to a farmer in Strabane at the wage of three pounds for six months and continued to offer his services in Tyrone farms till he was sixteen. Then he went to Scotland to work as a farm hand, a building labourer and as a coalminer at Denny in Stirlingshire. It was while he was in Scotland that he first discovered the value of the Co-operative movement. He became a member of the Co-op at Pumpherston, a town south of Edinburgh, and was able to save enough money to buy a farm at Cleendra. It was Æ who, spreading the gospel of cooperation, first gave The Cope the idea of setting up a cooperative society in the Rosses. He met with great opposition from the traders who had for years worked an unofficial cartel and whose monopoly looked now to be broken. They threatened to evict any of their debtors who joined the movement and indeed carried out their threats, unlike the local landlord who had never evicted any of his tenants. Their power was great: they had the law on their side and they had among their members justices of the peace. They also seemed to have the absolute support of the clergy. In spite of this opposition the Templecrone "Cope" flourished, and by 1906 The Cope himself was made a JP. The gombeen men continued their campaign. The Cope was sent to prison for a month because he would not find bail for good behaviour imposed by a bench which comprised five traders and a RM. His sentence was quashed when a Jesuit friend, T Finlay, made the case known to the Lord Lieutenant. The society continued to prosper. In time it owned a large store which sold hardware and clothing as well as groceries. A pier was built in Dungloe and a ship, the *Glenmay*, was able to break the British blockade during the Troubles. It came in with every spring tide for six months. The Cope set up a glove factory which gave work to 150 women and its generator supplied light free to both Catholic and Protestant churches and lit the main street of the town. In its heyday the Templecrone Co-operative Society was the biggest in Ireland and it still maintains three large shops in Dungloe. The Cope was prevailed upon to write his autobiography, *My Story*, which was first published in 1939. It is a racy, often funny account of a lifetime of achievement. Paddy the Cope died in Dungloe in 1964.

Betsy Gray

?-1798

A semi-legendary heroine of the 1798 rebellion, Betsy Gray's origins are obscure; "Betsy, maid or made-up?" joked Jack McCoy who made a study of her in *Ulster's Joan of Arc* (1987). In 1888 WG Lyttle published *Betsy Gray or Hearts of Down* which he had first serialised in his newspaper *The North Down Herald and Bangor Gazette*. According to this version, Elizabeth (Betsy) Gray was the only daughter of Hans Gray, a widower who lived in Gransha near Six Road Ends in north Co Down. Betsy, her brother George and her lover fought at the battle of Ballynahinch (13 June 1798) and, after the United Irish defeat, fled but were overtaken at Ballycreen where they were killed and buried. An earlier account, in *A History of the Irish Rebellion* (1833), written by CH Teeling who fought at Ballynahinch, has Betsy Grey (sic) leave her widowed mother to join her brother, her lover and the men of Ards at Ballynahinch where all three perished in the retreat. Betsy died first, according to poetess Mary Balfour:

> But lover's, brother's sighs are vain,
> Even in their sight the maid is slain.

At the supposed place of slaughter at Ballycreen, a monument was erected in 1896, but two years later it was destroyed by unionists who objected to nationalists coming there on pilgrimage. Then the man who erected the monument, James Gray, claimed Betsy was the daughter of John and Rebecca Gray of Tullyniskey (near

Waringsford) and that she had been exhumed from Ballycreen and reinterred in the family burial plot at Garvaghy. But this theory does not fit with the fact that the main body of United Irishmen came from the Ards region in the east of the county; and that there is still to be seen at Gransha the remains of a cottage which in 1900 was inhabited by McClenaghan relations of the Grays. Perhaps the last word should be left to a contemporary balladeer who was in no doubt about the facts:

From Gransha, near to Bangor Town, with Wullie
    Boal that day she came;
Her brother too was by her side, inspired by
    patriotic flame,
And when the tide of battle raged and showers of
    bullets fell around,
Still in the thickest of the fight was noble-hearted
    Betsy found.

Sir Tyrone Guthrie

1900-71

William Tyrone Guthrie, the *enfant terrible* of modern theatre production, was born in Tunbridge Wells, Kent, on 2 July 1900 of a Scots father and an Irish mother who was a granddaughter of Tyrone Power the great Irish actor-manager; her home at Annaghmakerrig, Co Monaghan, was to play a major part in his life and his legacy to Ireland. He was educated at Wellington and St John's, Oxford and on graduation joined the Oxford Playhouse but stayed only a few months. He was passionately interested in the theatre and would have loved to have been an actor but his height of 6'6" was against him. He concentrated instead on play production and became one of the most famous directors of the twentieth century. However, his career began in radio in BBC Northern Ireland and he was one of the first to understand and write plays for the medium of sound. He was director with the Scottish National Players for two years, 1926-7, with the Cambridge Festival Theatre in 1929 and 1930 and made his London debut with a successful production of *The Anatomist* by the Scots playwright, James Bridie. From then on there was no gap in a busy career and no geographical bounds to his work. He directed with equal zest West End successes and classical theatre. His time at the Old Vic—1933 to 1946 (with occasional gaps)—laid the basis for Britain's National Theatre and in his time he moulded the careers of Olivier, Richardson, Gielgud, Laughton and Flora

Robson. When the war ended his girdling of the globe began. He did *Oedipus Rex* and *The Taming of the Shrew* in Helsinki in 1948 and 1949 and over the next twenty years was the most mobile director in the world. He put on three Ulster plays in the Opera House, Belfast as part of the Festival of Britain and directed in New York, Minneapolis, Stratford (Ontario), Sydney and Tel Aviv. He had married his cousin Judith Bretherton in 1931 and she shared his nomadic, almost gypsy life; once they lived in a tarpaulin-covered punt on the Avon above Stratford. Their London flat was almost uninhabitable, and when on his mother's death he made Annaghmakerrig his home, the life was rich and plain. His special qualities lay in the making accessible of classics to ordinary people and in the establishment of professional community theatres where none had existed before. His work with the Stratford Festival Theatre of Ontario with its arena staging and modern-dress Shakespeare dissolved not only prejudice against the "highbrow" in plays but also in communities of mixed religions. In 1963 he was asked to establish the Tyrone Guthrie Theatre at Minneapolis. It opened with a modern-dress *Hamlet* and *The Three Sisters* and has been a matter of civic pride and artistic success ever since. The Alec Guinness *Hamlet* of 1937 with cigarette-lighters and the courtiers at Elsinore wearing Thirties evening dress caused a sensation, but it gave a remarkable proof of the universality and timelessness of Shakespeare's genius. Yet a production of Jonson's *The Alchemist* in 1962 which had characters in shorty nightdresses listening to transistor radios was less successful because less acceptable. All his theatre work, both in drama and opera, was characterised by great life and outstanding choreography, and the ensemble was as important to the production as the principals. He was knighted in 1961 for services to the theatre. He served as Chancellor of the Queen's University of Belfast from 1963 to 1970. After the death of his mother in 1956 he began to spend more time in Annaghmakerrig and, concerned at the high rate of emigration, helped finance and run a jam factory in a disused railway station at Newbliss, Co Monaghan. It failed in 1971, the year of his death. He died at his Monaghan home on 15 May 1971. One of his last public pronouncements was a call to the warring sections of Ulster "to catch themselves on" and learn to live together. When Judith died on 25 July 1972 the terms of his will were fulfilled. Annaghmakerrig, supported by the Arts Councils of both parts of Ireland, remains as a retreat for the artist, a fitting tribute to a great man.

Robert Hart

1835-1911

Chief of the Chinese customs service for nearly half-a-century, Robert Hart was descended from a Dutch-Jewish camp follower of William of Orange who settled in the Lagan valley. Hart was born on 20 February 1835 at 42 Woodhouse Street, Portadown, Co Armagh, the son of Henry and of Ann (née Edgar). Hart's father was a distiller who moved to Culcavey near Ravarnette in 1842; influenced by his Wesleyan beliefs he turned from distilling to linen-weaving and by 1855 he had made enough money to buy Ravarnette House. Robert Hart was sent away to be educated, to the Wesleyan School, Taunton, Somerset from 1845-8 and then to the Wesleyan Connexional School in Dublin. From 1850-54 Hart was a student at Queen's College, Belfast, from where he won a nomination to the British diplomatic service. He was posted to China, at first as consul at Ningpo and then in 1858 as secretary to the allied commission at Canton. In 1859 he resigned so as to join the Chinese Imperial Maritime Customs. Having set the Cantonese customs in order, he was made Inspector-General of Customs for all China. As such he presided over a multinational staff and was directly responsible to the Chinese emperor. Hart had a great respect for the Confucian ethics of the Chinese and for their aristocracy of learning; he maintained that the country of four hundred million people would one day be much more powerful. In 1866 Hart journeyed home, accompanied as far as Paris by the first Chinese diplomats to Europe. At Ballintaggart House near Portadown he met Hester Jane Bredon whom he married in Dublin and with whom he honeymooned in Killarney before taking her back to Pekin. There she gave him two daughters and a son and then returned to Europe to supervise the children's education. For seventeen years Hart met his wife and family only on the rare occasions when he returned to Europe; one such occasion was in 1878 when he led the Chinese government's commission to the Paris Exhibition (where he met President MacMahon of France). Back in China, Hart was responsible for founding the Imperial Chinese Post Office in 1896. In 1985 the Chinese marked the one-hundred-and-fiftieth anniversary of Hart's birth with a special stamp. Hart was a strict, methodical worker but each day he took time to play the cello and to read Lucretius or Cicero. In the Boxer rising of 1900 his home and possessions were destroyed but he never felt bitterness against the Chinese and in 1901 he published *These from the Land of Sinim* in which he discussed how Europe should treat China. When he retired in April 1908 he wrote in his diary that "we have helped to keep China quiet and the dynasty on its legs." From the Chinese he received the highest decoration ever bestowed on a foreigner (Ancestral rank of the First Class of the First Order for three generations) and from the British a knighthood (in 1893). He returned home to the freedom of Belfast (as well as of London) and to a warm welcome in Lisburn, especially from his fellow Methodists. On 20 September 1911 at his home in Great Marlow, Buckinghamshire, Robert Hart died of pneumonia and was buried under a Celtic cross in nearby Bisham. In China he was commemorated by a statue on the Bund in Shanghai which survived until the Chinese cultural revolution.

Hamilton Harty

1879-1941

The greatest Irish composer and the best-known conductor of his time in Britain was born in Hillsborough, Co Down (4 December 1879). One of ten children of Annie (née Richards, of Greystones) and of William Michael Harty (of Limerick) who was organist to the Church of Ireland parish, Herbert (Bertie) Hamilton Harty acquired a love of music from his father and a love of rural Ireland from his surroundings. After short spells as organist at Magheragall and at St Barnabas', Belfast, he went to Bray, Co Wicklow (1896). There he fell under the influence of a man who was to become his great friend, Michele Esposito, the Neapolitan who taught piano at the Royal Irish Academy of Music and dominated Dublin musical life. Harty became a gifted accompanist and after meeting John McCormack at the Feis Ceoil became a friend and mentor. He moved to the larger musical world of London where he married the soprano Agnes Nicholls (1904). Though the marriage was not a success, her musical connections led to Harty's being engaged as a conductor, principally of his own compositions, of which he was prolific at this period (Irish Symphony, 1904; Violin Concerto, 1909; "With the Wild Geese," 1911; "The Mystic Trumpeter," 1913; many settings of Irish poems). Joking that British opera was "dying of TB [Thomas Beecham]," Harty concentrated on orchestral work, and after wartime service in the RNVR, he became permanent conductor of Manchester's Hallé Orchestra (1919). At the Hallé he perfected his technique of eye-contact with the players, brought the orchestra regularly to London (where it was acclaimed), and did much recording work. He was famous for his advocacy of the music of Berlioz. (Unfashionably, he saw him as "a great intuitive composer.") Harty resigned from the Hallé (1933) to conduct the London Symphony Orchestra. There he began to appreciate the modern music of Walton, and triumphantly toured America (as "the Irish Toscanini"). Taking his traditional holiday in Ireland (in earlier years on Lough Melvin to fish, in later years in north Antrim to walk), he was diagnosed by a doctor friend as having a brain tumour (1936). From then until his death at Hove on 19 February 1941 he found it more and more difficult to work. Harty composed (and conducted) one last piece, for orchestra and soprano, "The Children of Lir" (1939). Along with his other Irish work "To the Wild Geese," this was his most lasting achievement as a late-romantic national composer. Honoured by TCD and QUB—he gave his library and royalties to the latter—Harty was knighted in 1925. At the end of the 1939-45 war, his ashes were taken home to Hillsborough, to the village, province and land he had never forgotten.

Paul Henry

1877-1958

Paul Henry the landscape painter was born in University Road, Belfast on 11 April 1876, the son and grandson of Presbyterian ministers. His father underwent a crisis of faith when Henry was young, and after a journey on foot round Ireland during which he climbed most of the mountains, he returned determined to follow the Baptist faith and soon became a minister in that church. Henry rejected all religion, finding Belfast and the austerity of the family religious practice intolerable. Like his friends James Wilder Good and Robert Lynd* he was educated at the Royal Belfast Academical Institution, a school noted for its excellence, its tolerance and its lenity. Henry was apprenticed to the Broadway Damask Company as a textile designer but found the work too cramping and left to study at the Belfast College of Art where William Conor*, his fellow townsman, also began his studies. In 1898 he left for Paris and the famous Académie Julien where there were human models available all day and work was only commented upon if the student wished it. A fellow student was Constance Gore-Booth who afterwards became the Countess Markievicz and one of the leaders of the Easter Rising. Through her he became friendly with Yeats and the other luminaries of the Irish Literary Renaissance. He also attended Whistler's studio in Paris and studied under Alphonse Mucha, the famous painter of posters whose work is now so popular. Whistler was a strong influence, as were Cézanne, Gauguin and

Van Gogh. His own early work consisted mainly of charcoal sketches and it was not until he came home to Ireland that he found his true style, that of western landscapes so formal and so Whistleresque that they seem like abstracts. He left Paris in 1900 and shared a basement flat in South Kensington with Robert Lynd, where they lived, as Lynd recalled, on bread, jam and whiskey and often had not the money to pay the milkman. It was Lynd and his wife Sylvia who first introduced Henry to the west of Ireland. Lynd had been commissioned to write a book, *Home Life in Ireland,* by Mills and Boon in 1911 and got married on the advance The honeymoon was spent in Achill and the Lynds raved so much about the people, the scenery and the light that Henry took them at their word, went to Connemara and stayed eight years, finding at last the style and themes he wanted for his art. His pictures of Killary Harbour and other western landscapes are remarkable and he could when he wished do excellent urban studies too. His "Belfast" and his "The Customs House, Dublin" are not so well known as his rural and sea pictures but still very pleasing. He went to Dublin to live in 1920 and made a career of designing railway posters. He was elected a member of the Royal Hibernian Academy in 1929, and in 1951 wrote an autobiography, *An Irish Journey*, which showed the same lack of interest in dates and sequence that characterised his paintings. He did some portraiture, notably of his brother R M Henry, Professor of Latin at Queen's. He went blind in 1945 and died in 1958, survived by his second wife, Mabel Young.

Frederick Hervey, 4th Earl of Bristol
1730-1803

Frederick Hervey, the Earl Bishop of Derry, was born at the family home of Ickworth in Surrey on 1 August 1730, the son of the man pilloried as "Sporus" by Alexander Pope. He was educated at Westminster and Corpus Christi, Cambridge. He took orders when he was twenty-four and his ecclesiastical career received its first boost when as chaplain to his brother George, the 3rd Earl, who had been made Lord Lieutenant of Ireland, he was given the bishopric of Cloyne in January 1767. From there it was but a leap to the much richer see of Derry. One of the legends associated with his colourful character is that word of the preferment arrived as he was playing leapfrog and he resigned from the game saying "...I have surpassed you all! I have jumped from Cloyne to Derry!" He was now thirty-nine and already manifesting the virtues and vices that were to characterise the rest of his life. While at Cloyne he had drained a local bog, and now in the northern see he began to build roads and bridges, to refurbish the churches and to construct magnificent houses for his own pleasure. He increased the yearly income of his diocese by £13,000 by good accounting and not by rackrenting and made Derry the showpiece of the country. He was greatly admired by the people in his diocese; they had a soft spot for a prelate who used make his curates run races after heavy meals for the prize of a vacant rich living. He built the first bridge across the

Foyle, designed a town-house for himself and began the building of the two Irish mansions that are forever associated with his name: Downhill and Ballyscullion. The former, set on a windy cliff on the north coast, survived till 1857, and its shell in the demesne he planned is still impressive. The folly known as the Mussenden Temple may yet be seen on the edge of the basalt cliff above Downhill; Ballyscullion, never quite finished, slowly deteriorated after his death. While these mansions stood they had more of the character of museums or art galleries than houses, since he loved lofty rooms and was a connoisseur and an advantage buyer of art on his many continental travels. In 1779, on the death of an older brother, he became Earl of Bristol with a yearly income of £20,000 and ownership of Ickworth, which now became the main object of his aesthetic improvements. He was a liberal landlord, a vocal supporter of such unpopular causes as Catholic Emancipation, and a militant if rather overdressed colonel of the Irish Volunteers. His rival and detractor Charlemont* tended to regard his activism and his support of liberal causes as characteristic and merely perverse. After this foray into politics his public career petered out. Increasing ill-health and the Irish weather made him spend more and more time in Europe, making Rome his headquarters and generally avoiding France. He was a friend of the notorious Lady Hamilton and conducted an ill-advised public affair with the Countess Lichtenau. He neglected his wife and his family was kept short of money at Ickworth. Hence Charlemont's charge that he was a "bad father and a worse husband." Yet he still kept an interest in Derry affairs and engaged in detailed correspondence with his agent and kinsman Henry Hervey Bruce. He died in Albano near Rome on 3 July 1803. His body was shipped home to Ickworth wrapped up as a piece of sculpture. There he is commemorated by an obelisk subscribed by Derry friends including the Catholic bishop and the chief Presbyterian minister.

May Hezlet

1882-1978

The best known member of a talented golfing family, May Hezlet was born at Gibraltar where her father, Colonel RJ Hezlet, was a serving soldier. The whole family were enthusiastic golfers; her mother helped found the ladies' golf club at Portrush in 1892 and the Irish Ladies Golfing Union a year later; her sisters Florence and Violet, between them, were five times runners-up in the Irish ladies' championship and four times in the British championship; her brother Charles twice won the Irish amateur championship and was three times on the British and Irish Walker Cup team. May's achievement, however, put that of the other members of the family in the shade. In 1894, at the age of twelve, she cycled every day from her home to the links at Portrush where she was already playing off a handicap of sixteen. At the age of sixteen she reached the final of the Irish ladies' championship and was defeated by Miss Magill from the Royal Belfast club only on the 18th green. A year afterwards, in 1899, May won the Irish title at Newcastle where she defeated Rhona Adair from Killymoon by 5 and 4. At the same venue, a week later, she defeated Miss Magill by 2 and 1 to win the British championship. May Hezlet won three more Irish titles (1904-6) and two British titles (1902 and 1907). Her record of being the youngest winner of both titles still stands. In 1905 May Hezlet played against Margaret Curtis at Royal Cromer in the forerunner of the Curtis

Cup competition, and in 1907, at Newcastle, she (and her two sisters) were members of the seven-woman Irish team which won the home internationals for the first time. By 1908 she was playing off a handicap of +6. May Hezlet also wrote about golf, in the periodicals *Golf Illustrated* and *Irish Golfer*, and in *Ladies Golf* which she published in 1904. After her marriage to the Rev AE Ross, the rector of Portrush, she played no more competitive golf and she followed her husband to England and then to Tuam where he became bishop. When in her seventies and widowed, she used revisit Portrush and could be seen hitting a few shots on a quiet part of the links. Perhaps Ireland's greatest woman golfer, May Hezlet died on 27 December 1978.

Bulmer Hobson

1883-1969

Quaker, republican activist and economic theorist,
Bulmer Hobson was born in Holywood, Co Down in
1883 of a family who had come to the Moy, Co Tyrone
in Cromwellian times. In *Ireland Yesterday and Tomorrow*,
a book full of a pawky Ulster humour though written
when he was eighty-two, Hobson remembered Alice
Milligan* lending the books of Standish O'Grady, and
how Cuchulainn and Ferdia became "far more real than
the crude town in which I lived." A boarder at Friend's
School, Lisburn, he read, despite the objections of his
English teacher, the nationalist monthly *Shan Van Vocht*
and the writings of Wolfe Tone. Hobson was a visitor to
the house of the poet Anna Johnston and here he met
Douglas Hyde, Maud Gonne and John O'Leary. In 1900
he set up the Ulster Debating Society and, with William
McDonald, the Protestant National Society. The latter
organisation allowed him to make the acquaintance of
David Parkhill and together they founded the Ulster
Literary Theatre to produce "distinctively Ulster plays."
Another cultural involvement of Hobson's was with the
Gaelic League; in 1901 he joined the Tír na nÓg branch.
Hobson was a nationalist in his sporting involvement
too, joining the Gaelic Athletic Association and becoming
first secretary of the Antrim county board. But then,
dissatisfied with the association's treatment of young
players, Hobson resigned and gave his time to the
founding of a youth organisation, Na Fianna Éireann.

Around this time, at a Glens of Antrim feis, he met and befriended Roger Casement*. In 1904 Hobson's political involvement began when Denis McCullough, the Belfast republican, recruited him into the Irish Republican Brotherhood. The pair were part of a group of young puritans who despised the inactivity of older republicans. They set up the Dungannon Clubs in 1905 and Hobson was involved in recruiting for them. He had trained in a Belfast printing house (1901-3) and he used his talents to establish and edit *The Republic* (1906); in James Good, Robert Lynd* and PS O'Hegarty, he recruited the most able journalists in Belfast. In 1907 Hobson was chosen to go to the USA to explain the policies of Sinn Féin, another nationalist organisation with which he was involved; there he met John Devoy and spoke in New York, Chicago, Boston and St Louis. On his return Hobson became involved in republican activity at a higher level and so he found himself living more often in Dublin. There he helped Countess Markievicz re-establish Na Fianna (which had lapsed after Hobson's departure from Belfast) as a youth organisation from which to recruit for the IRB. In the IRB Hobson was Leinster representative on the supreme council by 1912; he was also editor of the IRB paper *Irish Freedom*. Acting on IRB orders, he arranged the Rotunda meeting in November 1913 at which the Irish Volunteers were set up in imitation of the Ulster Volunteers. When the IRB lost control of the Irish Volunteers (to Redmond and the constitutional nationalists) Hobson was blamed and demoted from the IRB supreme council. Nevertheless the IRB used his talents to organise the reception of the rifles and ammunition landed at Howth (July 1914); later he gleefully recounted negotiating at length with the officer of an RIC detachment while his volunteers disappeared into the surrounding fields. Hobson believed in a policy of civil resistance, using the volunteers only in a guerrilla defensive role, and so he did all he could to prevent "a small junta within the IRB" planning an uprising at Easter 1916; the only result was that he was held incommunicado by more militant republicans from Good Friday to Easter Monday evening to prevent him interfering. So ended Hobson's political involvement; instead he became interested in economic policy and in the theatre. In the newly independent state he worked in the Revenue Commission from 1922-48 before he retired, first to Roundstone, Co Galway and then to Castleconnell, Co Limerick where he died in August 1969. Even as a civil servant Hobson showed independence of mind and trenchantly criticised aspects of state policy in *The New Querist* (1933) and in *National Economic Recovery* (1935). He lamented "political separatists [who] proved to be economic unionists" and on Irish unity he felt the only policy was "...to make an Ireland so prosperous that Ulster cannot afford to stay out of it."

Jemmy Hope

1764-1853

Linen weaver and United Irish revolutionary, James (Jemmy) Hope was born on 25 August 1764, at Templepatrick, Co Antrim, of a father who left his native Scotland rather than deny his Covenanter faith. He left school at the age of ten and was hired to William Bell, a farmer who insisted that his young charge listen to stories from Greek and Roman history after the day's work was done. This experience and his love of the Bible spurred Hope to learn to write. His reading led him to the belief that "The Most High is Lord of the soil; the cultivator is His tenant," and that landlords who abused this relationship caused misery. Resolving to change the system, Hope, by now a linen weaver, joined the local United Irishmen branch in 1795. Soon he represented it on the central committee in Belfast where he met Thomas Russell, Samuel Neilson and Henry Joy McCracken*. Hope and McCracken became good friends and they worked together recruiting Presbyterian tenants and farm labourers to the United Irishmen. Hope also recruited in the Liberties of Dublin where he worked for a period as a cotton weaver. Returning to Belfast in 1798, he realised that many of the better-off, "men who unthinkingly staked more than was really in them," were deserting the United Irish movement. However, Jemmy Hope remained faithful to the ideal and led a detachment of weavers and labourers in McCracken's army of 500 which marched on Antrim town on 6 June

1798. When they were driven back by General Nugent's much larger force, Jemmy Hope loyally followed McCracken into hiding in the hills above Belfast. When McCracken's sister Mary Ann came secretly to Bowhill to arrange a passage to America for her brother, Hope was still among his small band of faithful companions. After McCracken's capture, Hope managed to evade arrest and make his way to Dublin. He became involved in Robert Emmet's plans for an insurrection and in 1803 travelled with Thomas Russell to Belfast to see what could be done there. But the North had turned its back on revolution and Hope was lucky to escape the fate of Russell, who was captured and executed. Hope again went back to Dublin with his family, where he remained until the political amnesty of 1806. It was now safe for him to return to Belfast where for a while he was employed in the mill of John McCracken, brother of Hope's old comrade, Henry Joy. Jemmy Hope lived on in obscurity until 1853, when he died and was buried at Mallusk, Co Antrim. A headstone was placed over his grave by Mary Ann McCracken* and by RR Madden, who in *The United Irishmen, their Lives and Times* (1843-6) helped keep alive the memory of Jemmy Hope, the Antrim weaver who believed that "the condition of the labouring class was the fundamental question at issue between the rulers and the people."

John Hughes
1797-1864

John Joseph Hughes, the first archbishop of New York, was born on 24 June 1797 at Annaloghan, Co Tyrone. He was educated at local schools and followed his father to America in 1817 with the firm intention of becoming a priest. Hughes worked first as a labourer in Chambersburg, Pennsylvania and later became a gardener at Mount St Mary's seminary at Emmitsburg, Maryland. At the age of twenty-three he was admitted there as a clerical student. He was ordained for the Philadelphia diocese and worked in several city parishes. While in Philadelphia he founded the *Catholic Herald* newspaper and became known as an vigorous defender of Catholicism. In 1838 he was ordained coadjutor to John Dubois, Bishop of New York, and succeeded him in 1842. When New York became an archdiocese in 1850 he was the natural candidate to become the first archbishop. His period as bishop was notable for his reduction of church debt, his championing of parochial schools and his insistence upon government and local financial aid for them. Most significantly he checked the system of lay-trusteeism (the practice by which laymen tended to assume control of church property and have a say in the appointment of clergy) and strongly supported the rights of private schools. He fought the radical Irish press that had been established in New York by political exiles. He also advised Irish immigrants to stay in eastern cities where their religious needs would be catered for and was bitterly opposed to their following the spirit of the times and moving west. During the Civil War he was a strong abolitionist and became President Lincoln's special envoy to Europe to state the Union cause and counteract successfully the Southern states propaganda in Rome, France and Ireland. In 1841 he established St John's College, which later became the Jesuit Fordham University. He was also the founder of the North American College in Rome and he laid the foundation stone of St Patrick's Cathedral on Fifth Avenue, Manhattan. He died in New York on 3 January 1864. Hughes's Catholicism was very much of its time. He was famous as a supporter of his countrymen in exile and as one of the architects of Irish-Americanism. He was also a great interpreter of religion in America to Europeans.

Otto Jaffe

1846-1929

The first and only member of the Belfast Jewish community to become lord mayor of the city, Otto Jaffe was born on 13 August 1846 in Hamburg. His father Daniel Joseph and his mother Frederiké had come from Germany to Belfast in 1850 to establish a linen-exporting business. One of a family of four boys and five girls, Otto Jaffe was educated at Holywood, Co Down, near the family home, and later in Hamburg and Switzerland. From 1867-77 Jaffe worked in New York before returning to Belfast to take control of the family firm from his brothers, John and Alfred, who had retired. He married Paula Hertz from Brunswick in 1879 and they had two sons, one of whom became a barrister and the other a London company director. Jaffe became well-known in Belfast as a shrewd sharp-witted businessman but also for being lavishly charitable. He was a member of the harbour board and a governor of the Royal Hospital. His knowledge of Germany and its educational system made him a valuable member of the Irish technical education board. A member of the senate of Queen's University Belfast, he contributed £4000 to fund a university physiology laboratory. Jaffe entered local government in 1894 as a city councillor and was made Lord Mayor of Belfast in 1899. During his term he raised £10,000 for dependants of those fighting in the Boer War and was knighted at the end of his mayoral year. He was later High Sheriff of Belfast, and again Lord Mayor in 1904.

Otto Jaffe was life-president of the Belfast Hebrew congregation which worshipped at the Great Victoria Street synagogue, established by his father in 1871. Between 1871 and 1903 the congregation had increased from 55 to over 1000, mainly due to immigration from Poland and Lithuania, and so a new synagogue was built in Annesley Street, near Carlisle Circus. Jaffe both paid most of the £4000 cost of the new synagogue and, in his mayoral robes of office, opened it in 1904. Jaffe and his wife further contributed to the Jewish community by setting up a modern school for Jewish children at the foot of the Cliftonville Road. He died in London on 29 April 1929.

Patrick Kavanagh

1904-67

Considered by many, including himself, as the greatest Irish poet since Yeats, Patrick Kavanagh was born on 21 October 1904 on a small farm near Inniskeen, Co Monaghan, the son of James Kavanagh and of Bridget (née Quinn). One of seven children, he was educated at Kednaminsha primary school before being apprenticed to his father as a shoemaker, and then given sixteen acres to farm at Shancoduff. Kavanagh "took to the poeming" and in 1929 walked to Dublin to meet Æ, who published him in the *Irish Statesman* and gave him *Gil Blas* and *Moby Dick* to read. Dissatisfied with Dublin, Kavanagh went to London where *Ploughman and Other Poems* (1936) and *The Green Fool* (1937) were published. Distribution of the latter, an autobiography, was stopped when Oliver Gogarty sued Kavanagh for writing: "I called on Gogarty and mistook his maid for his mistress." After "giving London a second try," Kavanagh returned to Dublin to live in a variety of digs and flats, all of which were within walking distance of Parsons' bookshop in Baggot Street, whose proprietor, Mae O'Flaherty, was a great friend. The poet from Monaghan frequented the Palace bar, where RM Smyllie of the *Irish Times* held court, and soon he was writing special articles for the *Times* and the *Irish Independent*. When the first issue of the *Bell* appeared in October 1940, Kavanagh had a number of poems in it. In 1942 he wrote two long poems: *The Great Hunger*, attacking the misery of rural life, and *Lough Derg*, in praise of the place of pilgrimage. Religiously committed and a personal friend of Archbishop McQuaid of Dublin, Kavanagh became feature writer and film critic of the *Catholic Standard*. A second collection, *A Soul For Sale*, appeared for sale in 1947, but then a wrangle about rights, involving Macmillan, Pilots Press of New York and Kavanagh's brother Peter's handpress (also in New York) meant that nothing new appeared in book form until *Come Dance With Kitty Stobling* (1960). Meantime Kavanagh earned his living by writing *Kavanagh's Weekly* which lasted thirteen issues, by broadcasting talks on the BBC Third Programme, by writing a column for the *Farmers Journal*, and by part-time lecturing at UCD. Kavanagh got the latter job through the influence of the Taoiseach, John Costello, who as a barrister had savagely cross-examined the poet in an earlier libel case. By the 1960s Kavanagh was at last recognised as an important writer. His *Collected Poems* (1964) and *Collected Pruse* (1965) were published. RTE gave him a column in the *RTE Guide*, got him to do a "Self Portrait" and made a documentary on his life (both for television). At last, he had "arrived at complete casualness, at being able to play a true note on a dead slack string." In April 1967 he married Kathleen Barry Maloney. But he had been ill with lung cancer for years and he died on 30 November 1967. He was buried at Inniskeen, the homeplace he had immortalised in his poetry but to which he rarely returned for more than a few days at a time. For nearly forty years he had been more at home in the streets and pubs between Grafton Street and Baggot Street.

Jimmy Kennedy

1902-84

James Kennedy, popular song-lyricist, was born in Omagh on 20 July 1902, the elder son of Joseph Hamilton Kennedy of the RIC, but was brought up in the north-coast seaside resort of Portstewart, Co Derry, the inspiration for at least two of his most famous songs, "Red Sails in the Sunset (1935) and "Harbour Lights" (written some time in the forties and taking its title from that of an English pub). He was educated at Trinity and did some teaching before becoming an officer in the Colonial Service. He began writing songs to while away the time in a boring job and scored his first success with two now-forgotten efforts, "Hear the Ukuleles" and "The Barmaid's Song" which brought him to the notice of Tin Pan Alley and the sheet music publisher, Bert Feldman. He became a "lyric editor" and had an astonishing success with "The Teddy Bears' Picnic" which sold four million records. Kennedy wrote the words of songs, always the inferior position: as someone once told him, "You can't whistle words!" But he is remembered for his songs "The Isle of Capri" and "South of the Border" while the composers Wilhelm Grosz and Michael Carr are forgotten. Yet stung by the sense of being "merely a lyric-writer" Kennedy composed the music of another of his popular hits "Roll Along Covered Wagon" himself, picking the notes out on his piano. By the outbreak of the Second World War he was regarded as one of the world's leading songsmiths and an intimate of such popular performers as Bing Crosby. He became a Royal Artillery captain after peacetime service with the Territorial Army and composed for the British Expeditionary Force the sadly optimistic song , "We're Going to Hang Out Our Washing on the Siegfried Line." Later he devised the novelty dance the "Hokey-Cokey" (originally "The Cokey-Cokey") which was a feature of all forces dances during the war and played its part in the victory celebrations at every street party. His closest army friend was Denis Thatcher, who spoke the eulogy at his memorial service. After the war he continued to work at his craft until teenage record-based pops all but destroyed the sheet-music business. He still wrote occasional popular songs for the more mature market, notably "Love Is Like a Violin" for the comedian Ken Dodd. He lived in America, as a tax-exile in Switzerland and later in Greystones, Co Wicklow. Jimmy Kennedy died on 6 April 1984 in Cheltenham and is buried near Taunton in Somerset. He was married three times and is survived by his third wife, two sons and a daughter. Such songs as "The Chestnut Tree," "Oh, Play to Me, Gypsy," "Little Angeline" and the ones mentioned above have broken out of fashion constraints and been assimilated into a folk treasury for which the showbiz word "standard" is somehow inadequate. He won two Ivor Novello awards for services to music, and was appointed an OBE in 1983, but the honour he treasured most was the honorary D Litt from the University of Ulster in 1978.

Sir John Lavery

1856-1941

John Lavery, the painter, was born in Belfast on 17
March 1856, according to his autobiography, *The Life of
a Painter* (1940), but accounts of his early days are often
conflicting and other sources give the date as the 20th.
His father kept a small and unprofitable public house
which failed when Lavery was three. He decided to
emigrate to America but the ship sank off the coast of
Wales and he was drowned. This tragedy was com-
pounded by the death of Lavery's mother three months
later. He and his brother Henry lived on an uncle's farm
at Moira, Co Down until he was sent at the age of ten to
live with an aunt's cousin at Saltcoats in Ayrshire. Lavery
endured this unpleasant existence for five years and then
ran away to seek work in Glasgow. He had a brief spell as
a railway clerk and thought of enlisting in the army but
came home to Co Down for two more years before
returning to Scotland to work as a retoucher for a
Glasgow photographer. He stayed with the firm till he
was twenty-two, learning his trade at evening classes at
the Haldane Academy of Art. By then he decided that he
had developed sufficient skill to become a professional
painter. He studied at Heatherley's Art School in London
and at the famous Atelier Julian in Paris. In 1883 he spent
the summer at the village of Grez-sur-Loing and painted
many pictures, especially the famous "The Bridge at
Grez" which earned him a respectable reputation among
his fellow artists. He returned to Glasgow in 1885 and

had a great success at the British Royal Academy with "The Tennis Party." Two years later a commission to paint the state visit of Queen Victoria to Glasgow made his name and kept him in commissions for fifty years. His first attempts at portraiture were not very successful but in 1890, while in London, he met a flower girl in Regent Street called Kathleen MacDermott whom he painted and whose portrait did win critical favour. He married her soon afterwards but she died not long after the birth of a daughter, Eileen. He moved to London in 1896 and established a reputation as a leading artist. He was a friend of Whistler, whose work influenced him strongly, and when the American died in 1903 he was one of the pall-bearers. In 1910 he married Hazel Trudeau, the widowed daughter of a Chicago industrialist, Edward Jenner Martyn, and she was both inspiration and stern critic until her death in 1935. She was a very beautiful woman; hers was the portrait painted by him which appeared on Irish banknotes from 1928 until the coming of decimal coinage. His family now consisted of Hazel and her daughter, Alice, and his own child, Eileen, and he painted them many times. When war broke out in 1914 he joined the Artist's Rifles but he was now nearly sixty years of age and found he was no longer fit for army life. Instead he painted pictures of the Home Front, including the famous "The First Wounded" in 1914. He was knighted in 1918 and elected to the Royal Academy in 1921. The Laverys went to Ireland in 1921 and became friendly with Michael Collins. Hazel was one of the unofficial intermediaries in the Treaty negotiations. Collins visited them in their Dun Laoghaire hotel a few days before he was killed, and Lavery's painting of Collins's lying-in-state, called "Love of Ireland," has great solemnity. Lavery also painted Terence MacSwiney's lying-in-state and Roger Casement* in the dock. Other sitters were Bernard Shaw looking quite approachable in his London house, J M Barrie tucked into the corner of an inglenook fireplace and Cardinal Logue, small but aggressive. Lavery painted the marvellously atmospheric "Twelfth of July, Portadown 1928" specifically for the opening of the Belfast Art Gallery in 1929. Its capturing of the gaiety and the naïveté of the parade makes it one of the Art Gallery's most interesting pictures. He was careful to balance his gifts of paintings equally between the cities of Dublin and Belfast. He died at Rossenara House, Co Kilkenny, the home of his step-daughter Alice McEnery, on 10 January 1941. His body was temporarily interred in Mount Jerome cemetery in Dublin and after the war was placed beside that of his wife in Putney. His own daughter, Eileen, Lady Sempill had died in 1935, only six months after her stepmother.

Sean Lester

1888-1959

The first diplomat of the newly independent Irish state to rise to international eminence, as secretary-general of the League of Nations, John Ernest (Sean) Lester was born at Woodburn, Carrickfergus, Co Antrim on 27 September 1888. The son of Robert John Lester, a businessman, and of Henriette Mary Ritchie, he was educated at Methodist College, Belfast. In 1905 he began a career in journalism with the *North Down Herald* and then moved to Dublin where he became news editor of the *Freeman's Journal*. Lester was active in the movement for Irish independence and when the new state was set up, he joined the Department of External Affairs as a publicity officer. In Geneva, from 1929, he represented the Irish Free State at the League of Nations, a forum where the new state strove to play an independent international role. Lester successfully chaired a committee which settled a dispute between Peru and Columbia. As a result, in 1934 he became high-commissioner in Danzig/Gdansk, a city claimed both by the Germans and the Poles. There he showed great courage in refusing to be intimidated by the Nazis even when they had obtained a majority in the local assembly and begun to persecute the Jewish and Polish minorities. Eventually the Nazis made the League's position hopeless and Lester returned to Geneva to become deputy secretary-general of the organisation (1937). With the outbreak of war in 1939, Lester found himself in conflict with Joseph Avenol, the secretary-general of the League of Nations. Avenol believed a Nazi victory inevitable and opened negotiations with the French government at Vichy to make the League's palace at Geneva the co-ordinating centre for the new Europe. When Lester opposed these moves, he was supported by Adolfo Costa du Rels, the president of the League council, who made him acting secretary-general in place of Avenol (August 1940). For the duration of the war Lester presided over a powerless League staff who could do little other than preserve the organisation's records, in a Geneva where the Swiss government, under pressure from the Germans, made them less than welcome. Then, in 1945, at a meeting in San Francisco, dominated by the USA, who had never joined, and by the USSR, who had been expelled from the League, a new United Nations organisation was set up. To Sean Lester fell the melancholy duty of dissolving the League and disposing of its assets. Honoured by a Woodrow Wilson Foundation award, by degrees from both Dublin universities, and by the presidency of the Permanent Norwegian-Swiss Conciliation Committee, Lester retired to Recess, Co Galway to fish and to garden. He had married Elizabeth Ruth Tyrrell in 1920, by whom he had three daughters. He died on 13 June 1959 in Galway.

C S Lewis

1898-1963

Cyril Staples Lewis, the novelist, critic and popular writer
on religious matters, was born at Dundela, Belfast on 29
November 1898, the son of a police-court solicitor. His
mother died when he was nine and almost immediately
he joined his brother Warren in an English prep school.
"Warnie" and he were to live together for the rest of their
lives and slowly but surely oust their father (whom they
jibingly nicknamed "the P'daytabird" because of his
Belfast pronunciation of the word "potato") from any
"family" circle that they devised for their own comfort.
Lewis had been nicknamed "Jack" as a child and he
remained Jack to his friends He never used his hated
forenames except as initials on publications. The death
of the beloved mother and his subsequent misery first
brought to Lewis's attention what he later called the
"problem of pain." It was to become a recurring theme
of his religious writings. But first he went through a
period of agnosticism. (It was not until 1931 that he
again became a full member of the Anglican communion.)
His studies at University College, Oxford were interrupted
by war service with the Somerset Light Infantry at Arras
during which he captured sixty Germans and was
wounded. He returned to Oxford to read Classics,
Philosophy and English in all of which he got Firsts. He
set up a joint home with Janie Moore, the mother of a
dead army friend—a household which eventually
included Maureen, Mrs Moore's daughter, and Warnie.

For thirty years this ménage cost him dear both financially and emotionally. He was made a fellow of Magdalen College in 1925 and gained a deserved reputation as an excellent lecturer and a splendid if somewhat bullying teacher. He and his friends, Hugo Dyson, J R R Tolkien and Charles Williams formed a *conversazione* which they called "The Inklings". They met regularly to read their work in progress to each other. His most famous work of scholarship was *The Allegory of Love* (1936), a discussion on the interrelation in the Middle Ages between literary form and the development of passionate and romantic love, which won him the Hawthornden Prize. He also wrote the third volume of the *Oxford History of English Literature* (1954). Before this he had made his name with a science fiction trilogy with allegorical overtones, *Out of the Silent Planet* (1938), *Perelandra* (1943) and *That Hideous Strength* (1945). His book *The Problem of Pain* (1940) was very popular though some of his cynical colleagues remarked that the problem of pain was bad enough without Lewis making it worse. His diabolical correspondence *The Screwtape Letters* (1942) was a best seller. In 1954 Lewis moved to Cambridge as incumbent of the first Chair of Medieval and Renaissance Literature and by then was a well-known children's writer because of the seven "Narnia" books. In 1956 he married Joy Davidman, an American divorcée who soon afterwards developed bone cancer. Yet because of what seemed to the practising Christian in Lewis a miracle, a remission of symptoms gained them three years of blissful happiness. She died of the disease in 1960, by which time Lewis himself was in the grip of the osteoporosis which killed him on Friday, 22 November, 1963, coincidentally the day of the assassination of President Kennedy and of the death of Aldous Huxley. Lewis's ebullience, his male chauvinism and his "talking for victory" earned him as many enemies as his better qualities won him friends. Yet he was a man who faced the contradictions in his make-up with humility. His beautifully written spiritual autobiography *Surprised by Joy* (1954) is still a very moving book.

Robert Lynd

1879-1949

Robert Wilson Lynd, one of the finest of modern essayists, was born in Belfast on the 20 April 1879, the second child of seven and elder of two sons of the Rev Robert J Lynd, a leading minister of the Presbyterian church. He was educated at the Royal Belfast Academical Institution and Queen's College (later Queen's University) and began a career in journalism which lasted until a few months before his death. While at Queen's he became a socialist, an admirer of James Connolly and an Irish republican. He was a friend of Bulmer Hobson* and the main contributor to the latter's journal *The Republic* (1906-7). He went to London in 1901 and lived precariously on free-lance journalism until he became assistant to the literary editor of the *Daily News* in 1908. He was appointed literary editor in 1913 and remained with the paper (which became the *News Chronicle* in 1930) until 1949. In 1913 he began contributing a weekly essay, as "YY", to the left-wing journal which became known as the *New Statesman*. It was these weekly disquisitions which made his fame and which, printed in almost yearly volumes, made him one of the best-known journalists of his time. He also contributed to the popular literary journal *John O'London's Weekly*. Though Lynd lived in London for all of his working life, except for wartime evacuation, he remained a lover of Ireland and a fervent nationalist. He learned Irish and later became a teacher of the language. It was at Gaelic League classes in Oxford Street that he met his wife Sylvia Dryhurst and when two daughters, Sigle and Máire, were born in 1910 and 1912, Irish was their first language. Sylvia was a student at the Slade School when they met and afterwards became a novelist, critic and well-regarded poet. At the Irish classes he became friendly with Roger Casement* and, though a fervent supporter of non-violent Griffithism, the original Sinn Féin movement, he was active in trying to gain Casement a reprieve from the death sentence imposed for his part in the Easter rising of 1916. Lynd was a superb critic, a man keenly interested in sport and was known because of his generosity as "the softest touch in Fleet Street." The Lynds' home in Hampstead was famous for its literary evenings at which many of the leading writers of the day were likely to be present. It was to the Lynd household that James Joyce and Nora Barnacle came to celebrate their marriage on 4 July 1931. Lynd published in all thirty books, mainly of essays, which might be categorised as books about Ireland, books about writers and books about life. From the end of the first world war his books were usually reprints of his *New Statesman* essays. They represented the last great flourish of the form and with such titles as "Bus Tickets," "Aunts," and "In Defence of Pink" dealt in gentle wisdom and humour with the inconsequentiality of daily life. Lynd died of emphysema on 6 October 1949 and was buried in Belfast city cemetery.

Robert McCarrison

1878-1960

A medical scientist who became a world authority on the causes of goitre, Robert McCarrison was born at Portadown on 15 March 1878 and named after his father, a flax-buyer from Lisburn who had married Agnes McCullagh. McCarrison studied medicine at Queen's College, Belfast and at the Richmond Hospital, Dublin, taking a first-class honours MD in 1900. At the time Irish medical schools produced far more doctors than the country could employ and so McCarrison, like many others, looked for a job abroad. He joined the Indian Medical Service and set sail for what was Britain's largest imperial possession. The young Ulster doctor was stationed at Chitral, 1902-4, where he was regimental officer, and then as agency surgeon at Gilgit, 1904-11. In Gilgit, at the foot of the Himalayas, goitre and cretinism were endemic, except in one village. McCarrison was intrigued. He noticed the spared village had a pure spring water supply. He added suspended matter from the surface stream which supplied the other villages, to the spring and then had volunteers, including himself, drink the water. He had discovered that impure water enhanced iodine deficiency, so causing goitre. McCarrison, still in India and working at the Pasteur Institute at Coonor, became an expert on goitre and in 1914 was awarded the Prix Amussat by the Académie de Médecine in Paris. The 1914-18 war, and a period as an invalid in England afterwards, interrupted McCarrison's research. But by

1921 he was well enough to make a lecture tour of North America and to return to India in 1922. The prevailing economic climate was bleak, but after a dogged fight, McCarrison was given some government finance and made director of the Nutrition Research Laboratories at Coonor. There he pursued a programme of laboratory experimentation and field observation to ascertain the pathological effects of faulty food on the animal body, and then applied his findings to the study of human malnutrition. Though McCarrison was knighted in 1933, the importance of his work was only properly appreciated after Indian independence when that country's young scientists made a major contribution to a *festschrift* presented to McCarrison on his seventy-fifth birthday. By then he had retired from India (1935) and gone to live in Oxford where he was first director of post-graduate medical education (1945-55). He married Helen Stella Johnston, the daughter of an Indian civil servant, but they had no children. Robert McCarrison died at Oxford on 18 May 1960.

Henry Joy McCracken

1767-98

Best remembered of all the Ulstermen who strove "to forward a brotherhood of affection, an identity of interest, a communion of rights and an union of power among Irishmen of all religious persuasions," Henry Joy McCracken was born at High St, Belfast on 31 August 1767. His father John McCracken, a ship's captain, had married Ann, one of the Joy family who owned both a linen business and the *Newsletter* newspaper. As a young man, Henry Joy was apprenticed to the linen trade but he was not a success in business and it was probably because of his incompetence that the Joy, Holmes and McCracken cotton printing mill on the Falls failed in 1795. By then McCracken was deeply involved in the affairs of the Society of United Irishmen which had been founded in Belfast in 1791 by Thomas Russell, in imitation of the French revolutionary clubs. Government repression forced the society to secrecy and in March 1795 McCracken was sworn a member of the Tenth Society of the United Irishmen of Belfast. He recruited for the society among the Defenders (a Catholic agrarian organisation) in Co Armagh and even as far afield as Co Offaly. McCracken was with Wolfe Tone, Russell, Neilson and the Simms brothers when in June 1795 on Cavehill they swore "a solemn obligation" to work for Ireland. In 1796 the government attempted militarily to coerce Ulster, and McCracken was among those arrested and incarcerated without trial. From "Kilmainham Bastille" he wrote to his sister Mary Ann* of his hatred of being cooped up. Released on bail on 8 December 1797, McCracken resumed his life of restless activity, recruiting, planning, attending meetings. He and Robert Hunter were the Ulster delegates to the meeting of the executive in Dublin in May 1798, which decided to attempt a rising. While the Ulster leaders cautiously awaited the agreed signal, which never came because the Dublin leaders had been arrested, McCracken was, according to Hunter, one of the "violent young men who...attempted to bring out the People." Dating his proclamation "The First Year of Liberty, 6 June 1798," he called for a march on Antrim town. With a much reduced band of supporters, he captured the county town but was then driven off by General Nugent's superior force. He and a few comrades remained in hiding on Cavehill and Bowhill to the north of Belfast. There his sister Mary Ann visited him and arranged for him to take ship to America. While on his way to embark on 8 July 1798, McCracken was arrested by the Carrickfergus yeomanry. Brought to Belfast, he was quickly tried and, when he refused to inform on his comrades, sentenced to death. On 17 July 1798 he was hanged before the people of Belfast, who had by then deserted the revolutionary ideal. His body was taken by his faithful sister to be buried in the parish cemetery, on the road to Antrim. His comrade Jemmy Hope* escaped arrest and lived to recall that "when all our leaders deserted us, Henry Joy McCracken stood alone faithful to the last."

Mary Ann McCracken

1770-1866

A great radical Belfastwoman, Mary Ann McCracken was born in High Street, Belfast on 8 July 1770. She was one of seven children of John McCracken, a ship's captain, and of Ann (née Joy, of the family who owned the *Newsletter* and a linen firm). Mary Ann attended David Manson's co-educational school from which she graduated with a love of mathematics and of modern literature; the former she put to use in a muslin business she established with her sister Margaret; the latter to reading Mary Wollstonecroft's *The Vindication of the Rights of Women*. Believing that her age would "produce some women of sufficient talents to inspire the rest with a genuine love of liberty," Mary Ann McCracken became involved in every worthwhile cause. When Edward Bunting*, who lodged with the McCrackens, helped organise a festival to record the ancient harp music of Ireland, Mary Ann gave him every encouragement. Politically she believed in rights for Catholics and a democratic Irish parliament, and she supported the United Irishmen movement to which three of her brothers belonged. She was a friend of Wolfe Tone, who stayed in the McCracken home, while on his way to France via the USA in 1795. When her brother Henry Joy* (Harry) was imprisoned at Kilmainham by a government determined to stamp out the revolutionary movement, Mary Ann corresponded with and visited him. After the abortive insurrection of 1798, she succoured Harry, both while he was on the run, and when he was captured and sentenced to death. She did the same for Thomas Russell after the further attempt at revolution of 1803. From then on Mary Ann McCracken accepted that revolutionary feeling was at an end in Belfast, so she gave herself to a number of causes where she felt she could be of use. From March 1814 she was a member of the ladies' committee of the Poorhouse. However, her best work for the poor was done as secretary of the Belfast Charitable Society (1832-51), in which she was inspired by hearing Elizabeth Fry talk during her visit to Belfast. Other causes which claimed Mary Ann's interest were the committee to abolish the use of boy chimney sweeps and the association to help victims of the 1845-7 famine. She spent her final years in the home of Maria, Harry's illegitimate daughter whom Mary Ann had reared after her brother's execution. From there she corresponded with Samuel Madden who was compiling a history of the United Irishmen; it was Mary Ann's information which helped make Madden's portrait of Henry Joy so compelling for a later generation. And there, secure in the Presbyterian faith which had inspired so much of her activity, she died, aged ninety-six, on 26 July 1866.

Somhairle Buí Mac Domhnaill

c.1505-90

Somhairle Buí Mac Domhnaill, (*anglice* Sorley Boy MacDonnell), the Antrim chieftain of Scots descent, was born probably in the year 1505 at Dunanayne Castle, Ballycastle, Co Antrim. His early training was as a soldier and like most of his North Antrim countrymen, he regarded the North Channel as a mere ditch easily to be leapt. Most of his soldiers were Scots. He first came into prominence in 1551, when he was imprisoned by the Dublin government in one of their many attempts to expel the Hebridean Scots from North Antrim. On his release from Dublin Castle he seized Walter Floody, the constable of Carrickfergus, Co Antrim, declaring "playnly that Inglische men had no ryghte to Yrland" and held him to a heavy ransom. The native enemies of these Scots interlopers were the MacQuillins of the Route (that country round the present-day town of Ballymoney) and the Tyrone O'Neills, the premier northern clan. The MacQuillins were easily subjugated and Mac Domhnaill was made lord of the Route. Shane O'Neill ("Seán an Díomais") was, however, a much more formidble enemy. Both the MacDonnells and the O'Neills, woefully ignorant of *realpolitik*, tried to use the Tudors, particularly Elizabeth, to win local supremacy and at different times each made public submission. In 1564 O'Neill offered to rid the Antrim glens of the Scots and inflicted a severe defeat upon Mac Domhnaill at Coleraine in which Somhairle was severely wounded. The following year saw O'Neill holding the whole of Antrim and in an encounter at Ballycastle, Somhairle and his brother James were taken prisoner. James died in prison, his end, it was assumed, hastened by O'Neill. The clan wars continued. O'Neill was defeated by his enemy Hugh Dubh O'Donnell at Lough Swilly in 1567 and rather naively sought refuge with the MacDonnells at Cushendun. He was murdered there on 2 June that same year. For the next five years Mac Domhnaill spent his time mainly in the Isles consolidating his position and building up a fresh army. He had made some accommodation with the English but did not trust Essex. He met the English forces at Castle Toome in July 1575 and was defeated by Essex who then fell back to the garrison in Carrickfergus. Essex sent Norris to attack Rathlin where, it was known, Mac Domhnaill had sent all his treasure and, far more tragically, his wife and children and those of the other nobles. They were all massacred while Mac Domhnaill watched impotently from the Antrim shore. As Essex reported to Elizabeth he "...was likely to run mad for sorrow, tearing and tormenting himself...and saying that he then lost all he ever had." In spite of this terrible event Mac Domhnaill rallied, reconquered the glens and successfully attacked Carrickfergus. By 1584 he was in absolute command of most of Antrim and arranged for more and more Scots to come to live there. The English, now under Sir John Perrot, the queen's new Lord Deputy, determined to stop this growth of "a second Scotland" and moved against Mac Domhnaill. He, having made arrangements for the safety of his followers, again slipped across the North Channel to safety but was ready to sail when he saw the beacon light on Torr Head. He fought Bagenal and Stanley to a stalemate at Cushendun. After a lengthy impasse, another hop to the Isles by Mac Domhnaill and the capture of Dunluce from the English by an Irish troop, Perrot reluctantly agreed to treat with Mac Domhnaill. The Irish chief, now in his eighty-first year, went to Dublin and made a formal obeisance before a portrait of the queen in the Castle, which consisted of "kissing the pantofle of the same." He admitted he had no legal right to Ulster and lived in a kind of peace as constable of Dunluce and lord of the land between the Bann and the Bush till his death in 1590 at Dunanayne, the same house as saw his birth. He was buried in Bonamargy Abbey in Ballycastle.

James McDyer

1910-87

An apostle of self-help for rural parishes in the West,
James McDyer was born in the townland of Kilraine near
Glenties, Co Donegal, in 1910. He was the youngest of
seven children of John McDyer, a small farmer, and of
Brigid (the unofficial midwife to the area) who came
originally from Inishowen. In his autobiography, McDyer
remembered affectionately the values of a traditional
farming family: a feeling for religion, a republicanism in
politics, a love of reading. But he hated primary school
and felt "every child of my generation did likewise." At
St Eunan's, Letterkenny as a boarder, he regretted the
coldness between pupils and staff. He found that
Maynooth College also discouraged individualism, but
he made many deep friendships there. Ordained in
1937, McDyer was sent on loan to the English diocese of
Southwark, as curate in Wandsworth (and later in
Orpington and in Brighton). While there he was struck
by the English capacity for deep personal friendship, but
also by their suspicion of outsiders (in particular of the
Irish). In 1946 McDyer was recalled to the diocese of
Raphoe and sent as curate to Tory Island: at first he
begged to be sent back to England, but then he settled to
producing plays and trying to found a knitting industry
for his flock of 270. In 1951 McDyer was transferred to
Glencolumbkille, the place which was to become
synonymous with his name. Curate of an area drained by
emigration, with only five marriages a year, he resolved

to do something. First he had built, with voluntary labour, a community hall—a task accomplished in twelve weeks. Then he persuaded people of the value of electricity so that there were enough subscribers to make worthwhile the ESB's electrification of the glen. Using workcamps staffed by university students he began a group water scheme. McDyer made a number of attempts to revivify agriculture: a scheme to set up a central horticultural unit and piggery was rejected by the agriculture minister, James Dillon; a plan to make 112 small farms into one great communal farm of 15,000 acres was rejected by his successor, Charles Haughey; finally a project to grow and process 200 acres of vegetables was put into operation (but was later the victim of poor soil, bad weather and local fear of losing the dole by earning too much from agriculture). McDyer was more successful in expanding the traditional woollen industry of the glen. He managed to get de Valera himself to pressure Gaeltarra Éireann to open, in 1954, a handloom tweed factory which employed thirty workers. Later he encouraged the establishment of a hand-knitting and crocheting co-operative. In the early 1960s, McDyer, in a battered VW Beetle, travelled all over the West of Ireland addressing meetings of people who wished to copy his work in Glencolumbkille. In the course of his career he met strong opposition from some Fianna Fáil politicians but he remained outside politics, except when he joined the small group opposed to the EEC. McDyer's final involvement in Glencolumbkille was to set up a development association to buy the local hotel and to build a folk museum and holiday cottages. Unfortunately, disastrous losses by the hotel forced the liquidation of the association. Rugged, individualistic (but with a sense of humour), McDyer, looking back, felt it had all been worthwhile, even if some of his co-operative ideals had not been realised. By then parish priest, he died at the parochial house at Carrick, Co Donegal, on 25 November 1987.

Albert McElroy

1915-75

Non-Subscribing Presbyterian minister and radical politician, Albert Horatio McElroy was born in Glasgow on 14 February 1915, one of three boys of an orthodox Presbyterian family that had emigrated from Ulster. McElroy's early schooling was at Jordanhill College School in that city; but then his father returned to Ireland in 1930 to become sub-postmaster at Toome-bridge, and the youngster with a Scottish accent found himself at Rainey Endowed School in Magherafelt. From 1933-7 he studied French and English at Trinity College Dublin where, with Conor Cruise O'Brien, he helped found the College Fabian Society. While in Dublin he was won over to Non-Subscribing Presbyterianism (and to an interest in the ideals of the United Irishmen) by Rev Ernest Savell Hicks. During the years of the 1939-45 war McElroy served as a teacher and translator in the British army and met a Belfast schoolteacher, Jan McDougall, whom he married in 1943. After the war he taught in Ballymoney Technical School before going to Manchester College, Oxford, in 1952 to study theology. Then, in 1954, he came to Newtownards, Co Down as minister of a small congregation of Non-Subscribing Presbyterians. Inspired by a belief that those who "...led Ireland in 1798...derived their moral strength and integrity of character from their Presbyterian religion," McElroy entered politics. At first he joined the Northern Ireland Labour Party for which he stood, unsuccessfully, for election in Ards in 1945, and in North Down in 1950 and 1951. Then he was a founder member and first chairman of the Ulster Liberal Association (1956) where he felt more freedom to believe in a united Europe, a united Ireland as a dominion of the British Commonwealth, and a non-doctrinaire socialism. During the ten years to 1966 the Liberals strikingly increased the moderate vote in Northern Ireland: in 1961 Sheelagh Murnaghan won one of the QUB seats at Stormont; in 1966 the party won twenty per cent of the vote in the three constituencies it contested in the Westminster election, and in the Stormont election McElroy nearly won a second QUB seat. In 1967 the Non-Subscribing Presbyterians paid a personal tribute to McElroy by electing him as moderator of the church though many of them disapproved of his politics. By then the destabilisation of Northern politics which was to undo much of his work had begun. McElroy vigorously condemned the rise of what he saw as a bigoted Paisleyism, but refused to support the Northern Ireland Civil Rights Association marches, believing they would lead inevitably to violence. Having lost members to newcomers, the Alliance Party and the Social Democratic and Labour Party, his party saw its vote collapse in the 1970 Westminster election. Before he died, McElroy had the satisfaction of seeing direct rule proclaimed, and an election held under proportional representation to choose a power-sharing executive committed to co-operation with the Dublin government; but sadly for him there were no Liberals elected and the new government was soon brought down by a loyalist workers' strike. Albert McElroy died of a heart attack at his home, Brook House, Newtownards, on 13 March 1975 and was buried at Dunmurry Non-Subscribing Presbyterian churchyard. To the end he kept his belief that politics should be an extension of his Christianity.

Patrick MacGill

1891-1963

Patrick MacGill, the novelist, was born near Glenties in Co Donegal in 1890, the eldest of eleven children of a tenant farmer. He left school at the age of ten after only three years' attendance and worked at home until the age of twelve, when he was hired out to a Tyrone farmer. After a further two years he left to be a "tattie-howker" in the potato-fields of Scotland, back-breaking work which he described so graphically in his novel *Children of the Dead End* (1914) as "bad enough for men but killing for women." In spite of his limited formal education and the long hours he had to spend labouring in farms and navvying, MacGill became amazingly well-read and by 1910 had written *Gleanings from a Navvy's Scrapbook* which contained, as well as work-songs and poems of exile, translations of La Fontaine and Goethe. He had the book printed at his own expense by the *Derry Journal* and hawked it round the doors of the Clydeside town of Greenock. It made him famous as the "Navvy Poet" and led to an offer of a job on the staff of the *Daily Express*. The life of the reporter did not suit him and he gladly accepted the offer of a post working as an editor of ancient manuscripts in the library of Windsor Castle. The appointment was made by the archivist, the unconventional Canon Dalton, and it caused something of a sensation. When war broke out in 1914 he joined the London Irish and fought in the trenches in France. His experiences are recorded in a number of war books, notably *The Great Push* and *The Red Horizon*. By the end of the war he was much better known as the author of two best-sellers, *Children of the Dead End* (1914) and its companion volume *The Rat Pit* (1915). The first, admittedly autobiographical, tells the story of Dermod Flynn, his experiences as a migrant worker in the bothies of Scotland and of his abortive love of Norah Ryan; the second which necessarily overlaps the first tells Norah's more tragic story. MacGill had become the chronicler of the lives of his exploited people; the misery of the children sent into temporary bondage has seldom been better described and the account of the lives of the seasonal workers brought to an uncomfortable public an awareness of the exploitation. (A similar system of hiring-fairs and work in Scotland obtaining in the Rosses not many miles to the north of MacGill's country was the spur that drove "Paddy the Cope"* to found the Templecrone Cooperative Society in 1906, and Peadar O'Donnell* to attempt to organise the workers and seek better conditions.) The great famine of the 1840s was still a memory and the land, though slightly better in Glenties than in the rocky Rosses, could not support the many families that found their homes there. The credit system known as gombeenism meant that debts to the local traders were never paid off and the women's own form of bondage was to the knitting needle as in sweated labour they made gloves and sweaters for pittances. The Church had gathered strength after the famine years and some local clergy seemed in their own scandalous greed and in their public approval of the gombeen men to be exploiters as cruel as any. The lot of young and old was misery, and even if MacGill's anger rawly expressed diminishes his work as art, it gives it great power. It was labelled as "anti-clerical" at home and the exile described in his verse became a reality. He wrote nearly a score of other novels and a play called *Suspense* which was produced in 1930 in London, but apart from a comic novel *Lanty Hanlon* (1922) set in the Glenties district, they lack the skill and the raw energy of the two that made his name. He went to America in 1930 and because of a combination of ill-health and poverty never returned to Ireland. He stopped writing and effectively disappeared. He died in Fall River, Massachusetts in 1963. There has been a revival of interest in his work and the Patrick MacGill summer school is a regular feature of the Glenties August calendar.

Patrick McGilligan

1889-1979

One of those who played a major part in shaping the newly independent Irish state after 1921, Patrick McGilligan was born at Coleraine on 12 April 1889. The son of an Irish Party MP, he was educated at St Columb's College, Derry, Clongowes Wood College, and at University College Dublin where he studied law. Being naturally interested in politics, he joined Sinn Féin, the nationalist grouping in the ascendant after 1916. McGilligan stood unsuccessfully for North Derry in 1918 and had to wait until 1923 before being elected TD for the National University of Ireland constituency. From 1924-32 he was Cumann na nGael Minister of Industry and Commerce in the first government of a new state in search of internal security, economic development and external ties. McGilligan enthusiastically supported Thomas MacLaughlin, a young Irish engineer with Siemens Schuckert in Germany, in his scheme to generate electricity from the river Shannon at Ardnacrusha. In 1925 McGilligan signed a contract for £5 million and then established the Electricity Supply Board to run the hydro-electric scheme his numerous opponents saw as "the first fruits of Bolshevism in this country." After the assassination of Kevin O'Higgins, McGilligan was the most talented member of the government and he added the department of external affairs to his portfolio in 1927. He played a leading part in the evolution of the Commonwealth, both as a member of the committee on the operation of dominion legislation, and at the Imperial Conference of 1930; his reward was the Statute of Westminster which gave greater independence to Commonwealth countries and so allowed further Irish constitutional change. At the same time McGilligan expanded the Irish diplomatic network to Paris, Berlin and the Vatican and recruited the first cadets to the foreign service (one of the cadets, Frederick Boland, rose to become president of the United Nations general assembly). In the period 1932-48 McGilligan was elected by various Dublin constituencies on a platform of opposition to Fianna Fáil. At the same time he practised law, becoming a senior counsel in 1946, and was professor of constitutional and international law at UCD. In 1948, McGilligan's party, Fine Gael, was the major element in a coalition government; as minister of the notoriously conservative department of finance, McGilligan showed more independence of the department mandarins than any of his predecessors had done. In the second coalition government of 1951-4, McGilligan served as Attorney-General. He died in Dalkey in 1979, survived by his wife Ann, a daughter and three sons.

Seosamh Mac Grianna

1901-90

Seosamh Mac Grianna, one of the finest of modern Irish writers, was born on 15 January 1901 in Ranafast, one of the Rosses of west Donegal. His older brother Séamus Ó Grianna was also a writer, though more traditional in his language and preoccupations. The adoption by them of different versions of "Green" (their surname in English) is in a way symbolic of early distinction which led later to estrangement. He was educated at St Eunan's College in Letterkenny, St Columb's in Derry and trained as a teacher at St Patrick's, Drumcondra, qualifying in 1921. He taught at home for some time before becoming involved in the War of Independence. He took the anti-Treaty side in the Civil War and, like his brother Séamus and fellow Rosses man Peadar O'Donnell*, was imprisoned by Free State forces. On his release in 1924 teaching jobs were hard to find, so when *An Gúm* was set up he became a contributing writer and translator of (in some cases) pretty workaday books including English detective stories. *Muintir an Oileáin,* his version of Peadar O'Donnell's *Islanders,* is a notable exception. He saw himself as a full-time writer and wrote literary criticism in *Padraic Ó Conaire agus Aistí Eile* (1936), historical biography in *Eoghan Rua ó Néill* (1931) and a novel, *An Druma Mór.* This was submitted to An Gúm in 1933 but was not published until 1969, when a revival of interest in his work revealed the existence of the manuscript in the files. It was awarded a prize of £2000 by the Irish-

American Cultural Institute in 1971. One of the most poignant of his books is his last: *Mo Bhealach Féin* (1940). This autobiographical apologia contains the words which marked the end of his writing life: "Thráigh an tobar sa bhliain 1935,"[The well dried up in 1935]. His health gave way and the last fifty years of his life were spent mainly in hospital. Seosamh was strongly influenced by his mother, the "Máire" of his brother's pen-name, and he was determined to forge from the rich Rosses dialect a literary language that would speak for the new Irish state and give it the literature it needed for its fulfilment. Though Seosamh's stories are in the main set in his native place they are consciously literary. His first collection, *An Grádh agus An Gruaim* (1929), has stories which seem to show the influence of writers as different but as talented in the form as Daudet and Chekhov. It also contains a piece of historical writing in "Creach Choinn Uí Dhomhnaill" which, using a remarkably rich vocabulary, recreates 16th-century Ireland in so effective a way that one regrets that he never attempted an historical novel. He died on 11 June 1990.

Juan Mackenna

1771-1814

One of the best known soldiers of the Chilean revolution, Juan Mackenna was born John MacKenna on 26 October 1771 at Clogher, Co Tyrone, the son of William Mac-Kenna, of Willvale, Co Monaghan, and of Eleanor O'Reilly of Ballymorris. His kinsman, General Alexander O'Reilly, encouraged MacKenna to follow him into the Spanish army. Mackenna went to the Royal Academy of Mathematics at Barcelona in 1784 and then became a cadet in the Irish corps of military engineers in the Spanish army, in 1787. He served under General O'Reilly, first in the garrison at Ceuta, 1787-8, and then in Roussillon against the French revolutionary army in 1794. Though he was an able soldier, promotion was sl ow and so Mackenna, against the wishes of his family, sailed for Peru. There, under Don Ambrosio O'Higgins the Viceroy, he became governor of Osorno in 1797 and used his military engineering knowledge to erect coastal defences against a French revolutionary attack. But revolutionary ideas had already won over the descendants of the Spanish settlers. In 1810 Mackenna joined the revolutionary movement and became a member of the *junta* which José Miguel Carrera established in Santiago. Mackenna was made commander of artillery and of engineers. In 1813 he successfully led an army against Pareja's Spanish force, in southern Chile. But Mackenna disagreed with Carrera and supported a rival general, Bernardo O'Higgins, son of Don Ambrosio, who, when he ousted Carrera, made Mackenna his second-in-command. Unfortunately Carrera in his turn replaced O'Higgins and Mackenna was banished to Mendoza after being arrested in 1814. While in exile in Buenos Aires, Mackenna quarrelled with the dictator's brother, Luis Carrera, fought a duel with him and was killed on 21 November 1814. He was buried in the grounds of the convent of Santo Domingo at Buenos Aires. Mackenna married, in 1809, Josefa Vicuña Larrain, by whom he had a daughter, Carmen. Mackenna's biography, *Vida de D. Juan Mackenna* (1859), was written by his grandson, Benjamin Vicuña Mackenna, a well-known author in nineteenth-century Chile.

Charles Macklin

c.1697-1797

Charles Macklin was born McLaughlin perhaps in Derry but more probably at Culdaff in Inishowen, north Donegal. His date of birth has never been exactly determined but as he was traditionally believed to have been a hundred when he died his birth year is usually given as 1697. In fact the likely year was 1699. He was conscious of his Irish ancestry, boasting to Johnson's Boswell that if he could have proved himself to be the son of his father he might have claimed an estate in Ireland. His father died when he was still a child and he next appears as the stepson of Luke O'Meally, who kept a tavern at Island Bridge in Dublin. His first stage part was as Monimia, the female lead in a school production of Otway's play *The Orphan,* a singular piece of miscasting for the young McLaughlin was big and burly. Little is known about his early years but it seems that at the age of seventeen he became a strolling player in the west of England. Here he gradually lost his brogue and, despairing of anyone taking the trouble to pronounce his name properly, shortened it to Macklin. He became an established member of the Theatre Royal company at Drury Lane when he was thirty-three, with a reputation firmly established as a hard drinker and great lover. He had too an ungovernable temper; once in a quarrel over a wig he killed a fellow actor. He was found guilty of manslaughter and sentenced to be branded and discharged. The branding was carried out with a cold iron and Macklin reappeared on the stage of Drury Lane to tremendous applause. He continued to dominate the theatre of London and Dublin for fifty years and his greatest part was that of Shylock in Shakespeare's *Merchant of Venice*, which he first played in 1741. The couplet, "This is the Jew/That Shakespeare drew," which expressed the popular verdict is credited to Alexander Pope but it is unlikely that the invalid poet, who died in 1744, ever saw the performance. Macklin was the first to see pathos and dignity in the character which up till that had been played as a low comic part. He was Garrick's only rival in both comic and tragic roles and wrote extensively on his art in *The Science of Acting*, a book never published because the manuscript was lost in an Irish Sea shipwreck. He did much in his writings and his acting lessons to decry the tradition of stylised acting that was common at the time and introduced a "naturalness" which was regarded as revolutionary. He stressed clear and natural diction and the use of pauses to suggest intellectual turmoil and decision. Sometimes these periods of silent acting were rather long; once he berated an over keen prompter for interrupting "me in my grand pause." Macklin wrote ten plays including *The True-born Irishman* (1762), the very popular *Love à-la-Mode* (1759) and *The Man of the World* (1781). Macklin was married twice, first to an Irish actress Ann Grace and on her death to Elizabeth Jones who was exactly the same age as his daughter Maria. Macklin had lived with both women for many years before going through the form of marriage with them, but the man who is supposed to have lived in a *ménage à trois* with Garrick and Peg Woffington was no doubt able to take unconventional arrangements in his stride. Failing memory caused Macklin to retire from the stage in 1789 when he was nearly ninety. He lived for eight more years, dying on 11 July 1797.

Heber MacMahon

1600-50

Heber (alias Ever or Emer) MacMahon, bishop and general, was born in the barony of Farney, Co Monaghan in 1600. His father, Tirlogh, was of good family but he lost his holdings after the Flight of the Earls and lived in near-poverty near Killybegs in Co Donegal. He intended his son for service in Spain but his wife Eva O'Neill insisted that the boy be trained as a priest. So his education, which began in the Franciscan priory in Donegal, led to study at Douai and his ordination for the diocese of Clogher. This was at Louvain in the presence of John Colgan* in 1625. MacMahon returned to Ireland and worked for many years in his diocese, for most of them as Vicar-General. When Down and Connor became vacant in 1641 he was recommended by Archbishop O'Reilly as *optime aptus* for the see. He was accordingly appointed on 10 February 1642 but before he was consecrated bishop he was translated to his native Clogher and made bishop there on 2 June 1643. MacMahon seems to have had a struggle throughout his life between his clerical calling and a taste for politics. He is reputed to have confessed to treasonable practices during the period of Strafford's reign as Lord Deputy and was pro-royalist by the time that Ormonde became the king's minister in Ireland. He took a leading part in the Confederation of Kilkenny from 1642 and was Eoghan Rua O'Neill*'s chief adviser during the negotiations for peace in 1643, when Charles I hoped to use Irish support in defeating the parliamentary armies. In July of that year MacMahon's most compatible ally arrived as nuncio from the Pope. This was Archbishop Rinuccini. Well-briefed, he was prepared to let O'Neill be commander in the field but regarded MacMahon as the main defender of the faith. (Mac Mahon returned the compliment by writing to Rome and urging the Pope to make Rinuccini cardinal.) Ormonde concluded a peace with the Old English which MacMahon opposed because it did not guarantee religious freedom nor the restoration of confiscated Catholic property. There was a period of internecine squabbles; then the death of Charles I in 1649 and the landing of Cromwell in August that same year in a Dublin already ceded to the parliamentary forces by Ormonde, led to an *entente* between O'Neill and the Lord Deputy and plans were made to oppose the Protector. (Rinuccini had left in March at the request of the confederacy, despite having O'Neill's and MacMahon's support.) After O'Neill's unexplained death a fortnight later, MacMahon took charge of the northern forces. He captured the garrison at Dungiven, Co Derry and in a change from O'Neill's successful delaying tactics insisted on a pitched battle with Sir Charles Coote at Scarrifhollis, near Letterkenny, Co Donegal on 21 June 1650. The defeat was crushing, only the cavalry escaping in any numbers. MacMahon led his army towards Enniskillen, where in a skirmish with a party from the garrison he was badly wounded and taken prisoner by Colonel King, the governor. King tried to save his prisoner's life but Coote insisted upon execution. MacMahon was beheaded in Enniskillen and his head was set on a spike above the castle. His body was buried on the old monastic island of Devenish. He acquitted himself with exemplary courage on the scaffold and publicly accused himself of ambition and other sins. His nature was too fiery for the tasks he set himself but no one doubted his vigour or valour. Ormonde himself wrote, "These twenty years I had to do with Irish bishops. I never found any of them to speak the truth, or to perform their promise to me, only the Bishop of Clogher excepted."

Seumas Mac Manus

1869-1960

Seumas MacManus, the poet, novelist and oral storyteller, was born at Inver, Co Donegal in 1869, the son of a small farmer. He was educated at Glencoagh National School and qualified as a pupil teacher when he was sixteen. He taught in Enniskillen and Kinawley, Co Fermanagh, before returning to become principal of his old school at Glencoagh in 1888. He began writing early and had verse published before he was eighteen. He became a prose writer after winning a prize offered by the *Weekly Irish Times* for an essay with the title "A Ride in an Irish Jaunting Car." The area around Mountcharles where MacManus lived was rich in stories and folklore, mainly humorous, and on emigrating to America he discovered a ready periodical market for these essentially charming but authentic Irish tales. For many years he contributed material to American magazines then in their heyday, such as *Harper's, Lippincott's* and *Pearson's*. He kept in touch with his sources, maintaining a house in Mountcharles village and spending most summers in Ireland. His plays and sketches tended to be popular, light and humorous and his retelling of Irish myths and legends was very effective. He was in great demand as a lecturer and indeed as a kind of *seanchaí* and his store seemed endless. His best written work describes childhood in Donegal in such novels as *A Lad of the O'Friels* (1903) and *Bold Blades of Donegal* (1935). Some of his work was in Irish as well as English and he was one of the founders of the Gaelic League. He wrote a popular history of Ireland, *The Story of the Irish Race* (1921) and during the period of the Troubles was a constant defender of Ireland's position. In 1901 he married Anna Johnston, who as Ethna Carbery helped Alice Milligan* run the nationalist periodical the *Shan Van Vocht*, but she died only a year later. His second wife, whom he married in 1911, was Catalina Violante Páez of Venezuela. MacManus was appointed lecturer in literature at Notre Dame, Indiana in 1908 and received the degree of LLD (honoris causa) from the same university in 1917. *The Rocky Road to Dublin* (1938), a barely fictionalised autobiography, has the same gusto as his novels and stories. The hero Jaimie has adventures that follow MacManus's life very closely and ends with the characteristically titled chapter "And he lived happily ever after." MacManus died after a fall from a nursing-home window in 1960.

Louis MacNeice

1907-63

Louis MacNeice, the Irish poet who was a spiritual colleague of the left-wing "politicals" W H Auden and Stephen Spender, was born on 12 September 1907, as he put it himself: "...in Belfast between the mountains and the gantries," the son of John F MacNeice DD, who afterwards became Bishop of Down and Dromore. His early childhood was spent in Carrickfergus but true to his class he was sent first to a preparatory school in England and then to a public school, in his case, Marlborough. Here it pleased him to exploit his Irishness, because in the school stories he had read, "the Irish boys and girls... did what they liked and were always popular." He had to admit though that unlike the Irish of his stories, "I could not ride a horse, I had never poached a salmon, my background was pathetically suburban." He went to Merton College, Oxford and on graduation became lecturer in classics at Birmingham University in 1930. In 1936 he transferred to Bedford College in London as lecturer in Greek and in 1940 joined the famous Features Department of the BBC, which under Laurence Gilliam produced some of the finest radio programmes ever—in a sense defining the medium as an art form. He stayed with the department for twenty years as writer and producer, retiring in 1961 to concentrate upon his own work in poetry and drama. In 1963, while supervising the recording underground of scenes from his play *Persons from Porlock,* he contracted viral pneumonia and he died on 3 September. MacNeice wrote some very successful radio plays, notably *The Dark Tower*(1947), and though his writing for the stage was not in general so effective, *One for the Grave*, his modern Everyman, did well when it was produced at the Dublin Theatre Festival in 1966. It is primarily as a poet that he will be remembered. His long poem *Autumn Journal*, written at the time of the Munich crisis is one of the finest of its kind—apologia, chronicle and prophecy. He published in all nine books of poetry, including some of the finest of modern love poems and compelling verse about his native country to which he regularly returned as a theme for his poetry. As he wrote in "Valediction":

But I cannot deny my past to which myself is
    wed,
The woven figure cannot undo its thread.

Eóin MacNeill

1867-1945

A scholar and a revolutionary, Eóin MacNeill was born on 15 May 1867 in Glenarm, Co Antrim. He was one of eight children of Archibald MacNeill, a general merchant, and of Rosetta Macauley. The MacNeills were talented: James joined the Indian civil service, and later the Irish diplomatic service, becoming the new state's first envoy to London; Hugh taught Latin at University College Dublin and was immortalised as "Professor McHugh" by James Joyce. Eóin was educated at St Malachy's College, Belfast and the Royal University before becoming a law courts clerk in Dublin. Fired by the contemporary enthusiasm for Irish, he learned the language on Inis Meadhon, in the Aran Islands, and then joined with Douglas Hyde to set up Conradh na Gaeilge (The Gaelic League) in 1893. MacNeill wrote in favour of the revival of the language both in the *Gaelic Journal*, of which he became editor in 1894, and in *An Claidheamh Soluis* where he became founding editor in 1899. At the same time he earned his living by teaching Irish at Drumcondra Teacher-training College from 1897 until 1909, when he became professor of Early Irish History at University College Dublin. MacNeill's involvement in the language movement led naturally to an active involvement in politics. As a result of his article in *An Claidheamh Soluis* in which he declared that "a wonderful state of things has come to pass in Ulster [with the establishment of the Ulster Volunteers]" a meeting was held at the Rotunda in

Dublin on 25 November 1913 at which the Irish Volunteers were formed. As chief-of-staff, MacNeill saw the volunteers as a means "to win our rights by being ready to fight for them but without fighting." So he was shocked to discover that an Irish Republican Brotherhood/ Citizen Army grouping were secretly planning an insurrection, and he immediately called off the volunteer mobilisation planned for Easter Monday 1916. Amidst confusion the rising went ahead, and after its failure MacNeill was imprisoned in Great Britain until the general amnesty of 1917. In Sinn Féin's landslide election victory of 1918 MacNeill was a successful candidate for both Derry City and the National University of Ireland. The revolutionaries refused to sit at Westminster and instead set up Dáil Eireann, where MacNeill was in turn Minister of Finance and Ceann Comhairle (speaker). MacNeill took the side of those who supported the 1921 treaty with Great Britain and so was given office in the first Irish Free State government, as Minister of Education. But MacNeill was temperamentally unsuited to parliamentary politics and came to grief when he was appointed Free State representative on the commission to establish the exact boundary with Northern Ireland. MacNeill saw his function as judicial rather than political and was easily outwitted by the Northern unionist commissioner. The boundary remained that of the Six Counties and the nationalists who were in the majority in two of the counties were outraged. As a result MacNeill resigned from the commission and from the cabinet and, after being defeated in the 1927 election, from politics. He returned to academic life, becoming chairman of the Irish Manuscripts Commission, corresponding member of the *Académie des inscriptions et des belles-lettres* (1931) and president of the Royal Irish Academy (1940-3). In his written work, especially *Phases of Irish History* (1919) and

Celtic Ireland (1921), he used his knowledge of old Irish to deal critically with the sources and so laid a foundation for a scientific view of early Irish history. MacNeill married Agnes Moore of Ballymena by whom he had seven children. Remembered by generations of students as a tall gaunt bearded figure dressed in black, MacNeill died in Dublin on 15 October 1945. To the end he remained an Antrim man, proud that he could recite "Árd Tí Cuain" from memory.

St Malachy

1095-1148

St Malachy (in Irish *Mael Maedoc*) the reforming archbishop of Armagh and one of the few to come from the diocese, was born about 1095 near the present city. His parents died when he was young and he was nurtured by a hermit, Eimar. Ordained by Archbishop Ceallach at the age of twenty-five, he began the work of reform with which his name is historically associated. The main element of his policy was the final reconciliation of the Celtic church with Rome, the establishment of canonical hours and the bringing back of administration of the sacraments which had fallen into disuse. He attended the monastery of St Malchus at Lismore before his appointment as abbot of Bangor in 1123. His appointment to the see of Connor followed the next year, though he continued to live in the monastery and follow the monastic rule. Four years later in 1128 he and his monks were forced to leave Bangor because of armed opposition from a northern chieftain and they were given a grant of land in Kerry by the king of Desmond. In 1132 Ceallach died, naming Malachy as his successor, but owing to local politics he was unable to take his living until 1134. Even then the hereditary candidate had to be bribed to return the ancient staff of St Patrick and the Book of Armagh. When he had restored ecclesiastical order he resigned the primatial see and returned to Connor. Though the church was significantly reformed it still lacked formal papal recognition, so Malachy was sent to

Rome to seek the *pallium,* the lambswool collar that an archbishop or his delegate must receive from the hand of the Pope to confirm his archbishopric. On the way to the court of Innocent II he stopped off at Clairvaux where St Bernard had his Cistercian abbey. The two men became friends and after Malachy's death Bernard became his first biographer. His stories of the decadence of the Irish church were perhaps exaggerated because even Bernard wondered how so saintly a man could have come from a land so barbarous. The Pope decided that *pallia* would be conferred only at the request of a national synod, but he made Malachy papal legate to it. Malachy hurried home, taking with him enough monks to establish a Cistercian community on land granted at Mellifont. The synod was held in 1148 at Inispatric near Skerries, Co Dublin and Malachy was despatched again to Rome for the *pallia* of Armagh and Cashel but died on the way at Clairvaux on 2 November 1148. Bernard buried him in his own habit and wore Malachy's for the remaining five years of his life. By then the Irish church had been granted four archbishoprics instead of two.

Alice Milligan

1865-1953

Alice Milligan, the poet and nationalist editor, was born near Omagh in September 1865, the daughter of Seaton F Milligan, a wealthy businessman and antiquary who became a member of the Royal Irish Academy. She was educated at Methodist College, Belfast, Magee College, Derry and King's College, London but preferred to go to Dublin to learn Irish rather than accept her father's offer of residence in Germany to learn the more fashionable continental language. Her nationalism received a further boost when she began attending meetings at which Parnell was the main speaker. Her acquaintance with Irish had begun on visits to the farm of her great-uncle, Armour Alcorn, a farmer with extensive property who used Irish to speak to his labourers. Her poem "When I Was a Little Girl" in which she dismisses her nurse's terrors about the coming of the dreaded Fenians by thinking, "When the Fenians come/ I'll rise and go after," shows a very early tendency towards nationalism. She taught for some time in a girl's college in Derry and afterwards moved to Belfast where with her friend Anna Johnston (Ethna Carbery*) she edited first a Connollyite paper, the *Northern Patriot,* and then a less socialist-orientated and more nationally cultural journal called the *Shan Van Vocht.* After 1893 she was the main organiser of the Gaelic League in Ulster and one of her poems, "The Man on the Wheel," is a tribute to the many *múinteoirí taistil* who travelled the country mainly on bicycles to teach Irish to adults. The first event in which Irish was heard in a stage presentation took place in Letterkenny in November 1898 and characteristically she was one of the actors. *The Deliverance of Red Hugh*, which she described as a "Dramatic Incident in Two Scenes," was acted by Inghínidhe na hÉireann on 27 August 1901 and when it was published in the *Weekly Freeman* on 13 March 1902, she also supplied a version in Irish. Her play, *The Last Feast of the Fianna*, which was produced on 19 February 1900, was one of the first to be staged by the Irish Literary Theatre, the precursor of the Abbey. Alice Milligan's sister, Charlotte, who was an authority on Irish folk music, supplied specially-written music for the play and for *The Harp That Once* which was produced in Dublin in the Antient Concert Rooms on 26 August 1901. (Another play, *The Daughter of Donagh,* was produced at the Abbey in 1920.) In 1898 Alice Milligan was appointed organising secretary in Ulster for the centenary celebrations of the '98 rising and was able to bring several distinguished speakers to Belfast, including John O'Leary. Her *Life of Wolfe Tone* was written to coincide with the centenary. Alice Milligan was greatly affected by the civil war and the partition of Ireland. She was one of the founders of the Anti-Partition League and in some sense lost heart when it became clear that the reunification of the country would not be an easy task. She was honoured with a D Litt. by the National University of Ireland and died on 13 April 1953 at Tyrcar near Omagh. Her poetry was published in book form as *Poems* in 1954, not long after her death.

Jane Verner Mitchel
1821-99

The wife of a restless refugee revolutionary and mother of his six children, Jenny Mitchel was born in Co Armagh in 1821. She was the daughter of Mary Ward, who was herself the daughter of a coachman on the Church Hill estate of the Verners of Loughgall. Jenny grew up in Newry in the house of Capt James Verner, whom she considered her father; after his death in 1847, his brother Sir William Verner disclaimed the relationship, saying that Jenny was the bastard daughter of a local schoolmaster in Loughgall. In any case, Jenny was sent to Miss Bryden's school for young ladies and it was while returning from school that she met and fell in love with John Mitchel*, son of a local Presbyterian minister, who became famous as a nationalist writer. She eloped with him to Chester but was caught and sent home. A year later, in 1837, she married him secretly in Dromore, Co Down. Jenny set up the first of many homes, in a cottage at Dromalane, Co Down, near the Mitchel family home. Then she moved to Banbridge where her husband practised as an attorney. There she began rearing her first four children, Johnnie, James, Henrietta and William and regularly entertained her husband's friends, John Martin, Gavan Duffy* and John O'Hagan. In 1845 her husband moved to Dublin to work on the *Nation* newspaper and so Jenny and her four children moved, first to 1 Upper Leeson Street and later to 8 Ontario Terrace, near Charlemont Bridge. In Dublin she was hostess to her husband's Young Ireland friends, gave birth to another daughter, Minnie, and, in Green Street courthouse, saw her husband sentenced to fifteen years' transportation for seditious journalism (May 1848). Jenny's house was seized and she had to return to Newry with her children and wait for her husband to serve his sentence. When informed in 1851 that her husband was a ticket-of-leave man in Van Diemen's Land (Tasmania), she, five children and two servants set sail on board the *Condor* to meet him. Jenny and her husband settled at Bothwell in Tasmania where another daughter, Rixie, was born in 1852. In 1853 Jenny and her six children, accompanied by her husband, who was disguised as a Jesuit, sailed to New York (via Sydney, Tahiti, San Francisco and Nicaragua). There she set up home in Brooklyn after being toasted as "brave Mrs Mitchel" at an Irish banquet in Broadway Theatre. In Brooklyn she kept open house to all the Young Ireland exiles before following her husband to Washington (where he started a newspaper). In 1859 her husband joined revolutionary friends in Paris and naturally Jenny went too. They lived in Choisy-le-Roi. Her older daughters went to Sacré Coeur convent school, and one, Henrietta (Henty), became a Catholic and decided to enter the order; a postulant, she died in 1863 and was buried in Montparnasse. But by then Jenny was on her way to the USA, following her husband who had gone there to report on the civil war in which her son Willie was killed at Gettysburg and her son Johnnie at Fort Sumter (1864). While her husband was forced into exile in Paris after the Southern defeat, Jenny moved to New York. There she was joined by her husband, now stricken by tuberculosis, but still enthusiastic for Irish politics; in 1875 he returned to Ireland to fight an election and died there. Jenny never saw his burial place in Newry but his Irish-American supporters left her financially secure at last with a memorial fund of $30,000. Jenny lived to see Rixie and her first child die; her son James marry and give her a grandson; her daughter Minnie, with another grandson, leave her alcoholic husband and move back to Jenny's house in Brooklyn. Jane Verner Mitchel died on 31 December 1899 and was buried at Woodlawn Cemetery, faithful to the last to her husband, to his career as a revolutionary and to his children.

John Mitchel

1815-75

Young Irelander and chronicler of convict life, John
Mitchel was born on 3 November 1815 at Camnish
manse, Dungiven, Co Derry, son of Rev John Mitchel
and of Mary Haslett of Maghera. In 1819 Rev Mitchel was
"called" to Derry city and to Newry in 1823. There the
family settled at Dromalane, the father living until 1840
and the mother until 1863. Son John was educated at Dr
Henderson's school in Newry and later at Trinity College
Dublin (1830-34). Mitchel had difficulty deciding on a
career; for a while he was enthused by his father's "New
Light" Presbyterianism and wanted to become a minister;
then he worked for a period in his uncle William Haslett's
bank in Derry. Finally he settled on the law and was
apprenticed as a solicitor to John Quinn of Newry; later
he practised as an attorney at Banbridge. In 1837 he
married Jenny Verner, a seventeen-year-old with whom
he had eloped a year earlier to Chester. The marriage was
happy and she gave him six children. From 1842 onwards
Mitchel came under the influence of the *Nation* newspaper and of the Young Irelanders who thought Daniel
O'Connell too old and his politics too tame. Mitchel met
Thomas Davis who induced him to write a *Life of Hugh
O'Neill* as well as articles for the *Nation*. When Davis died
prematurely in 1845, Mitchel succeeded him as a
journalist for the *Nation* and went to live in Dublin, first
in Leeson Street and later at Charlemont Bridge. Though
he admired O'Connell's past achievements for the Repeal

Association, he was among those who seceded in 1846 to form the Irish Confederation. By 1848 Mitchel's position was so radical that he had left the *Nation* to found the *United Irishman*. Encouraged by events in Paris, the more radical Young Irelanders were contemplating a revolution. Before the great day came Mitchel was charged with writing seditiously and sentenced to fourteen years' transportation. He was sent via Bermuda to Van Diemen's Land (Tasmania) where his wife and family joined him in 1851. In *Jail Journal* (1854), a beautifully written account of these years, he described how he eventually escaped to the USA in 1853. From that time on, unable to return to Ireland and so restless and unhappy, Mitchel lived alternately in America and in Paris. In America he farmed for a while, then edited the *Irish Citizen* newspaper and wrote *The History of Ireland*. In the American civil war he sympathised with the agricultural and more romantic South against the industrial North, lost two sons in the fighting and was imprisoned for a short while by the victorious Northern forces. In Paris he wrote a "letter" for the Dublin *Irishman*; one of his despatches evoked Myles Byrne, a refugee since 1798: "Walking on some of these bright winter days along the avenue of the Champs-Elysée, you may see a tall figure, the splendid ruin of a soldier d'élite, bearing himself still erect under the weight of eighty winters." It was in Paris also that Mitchel watched a daughter Henrietta (Henty), who had become a Catholic, die while still at school. In 1866 his Young Irelander friends, John Martin and Fr Kenyon, came over from Ireland and they all visited the Collège des Irlandais where the old revolutionary was cheered by the students (despite the college president's disapproval). Mitchel revisited Ireland at last in 1874 and the next year a new generation of radicals had him elected M.P. for Co Tipperary. He was unseated as a "felon" but then re-elected. Mitchel had little time to savour the tribute to his incorruptibility. On 20 March 1875, he died in his beloved Dromolane and was buried beside his parents at Old Meeting House Green, off High Street in Newry.

"Rinty" Monaghan

1920-84

John Joseph "Rinty" Monaghan, world flyweight boxing champion, was born in the docks area of Belfast in 1920, one of thirteen children. He learned the fight game in McAloran's gymnasium in Hardinge Street not far from his home. Frank McAloran afterwards became his manager. He fought his first professional bout at fourteen years of age, knocking out his opponent in the fourth round. He quickly established a public persona which had as much to do with showbiz as with fisticuffs: his name came from the famous series of Hollywood wonder dogs, "Rin-Tin-Tin" partly because of his childhood obsession with the films and also because of the speed of his footwork in the ring, and it was his practice to conclude his (usually winning) fights by singing the popular Irish-American song, "When Irish Eyes Are Smiling." He first came into international prominence when he knocked out Terry Allen in London in March 1947 and later that year outpointed the champion French flyweight, Emile Famechon. At the time the world flyweight champion was Jackie Paterson of Glasgow. He was due to fight a Cuban challenger, Dado Marino, but was unable to make the weight in time for the bout. Monaghan stepped in and though deemed to be well ahead on points he was beaten on a foul in the ninth round. He won the return match against Marino in October 1947 and was recognised as world champion by one of the boxing associations. Paterson was reinstated as world champion the next year by the British Boxing Board of Control and he met Monaghan on 23 March 1948 at the King's Hall, Belfast. Monaghan knocked out Paterson in the seventh round and won the world title decisively. The crowd in the hall joined in the singing of the theme song that night. He defended his title twice, outpointing Maurice Sandreyon in September 1949 and later that year drawing with the London boxer Terry Allen. Monaghan retired undefeated six months later. In later years he appeared in pubs and nightclubs as a "singing boxer" but with no great success and reverted to his old job as a taxi driver. Later he worked as a petrol-pump attendant. He died on 3 March 1984 in Belfast, survived by his wife Frances and six children. He was the subject of a play, *Rinty*, by the Belfast playwright Martin Lynch which had its *première* at the Arts Theatre in his native city in September 1990.

Micheál Ó Cléirigh

c.1590-1643

Ó Cléirigh's career typifies the reaction of Gaelic Ireland
to the advance of English conquest, colonisation,
language and religion. The son of Donnchadh, one of a
family who were hereditary historians to the O'Donnells,
and of Honora Ultach, he was born c.1590 at Kilbarron
in south Donegal where he was christened Tadhg. Ó
Cléirigh studied poetry and history under Baothghalach
Rua MacAodhagain. Like many other young Ulstermen,
in the wake of the flight of O'Neill and O'Donnell, he
found himself in exile in the Spanish Netherlands. At
Louvain (now Leuven) the Irish Franciscans, because of
the destruction of friaries at home, had established the
Collège St Antoine as a base in which to train postulants.
About 1622 Ó Cléirigh followed his brother Myler into
the college where he became Brother Micheál. Two of the
community, Aodh Mac an Bhaird and Patrick Fleming,
were planning to write lives of Irish saints. They
recognised Brother Micheál's abilities and despatched
him to Ireland in 1626 to collect material. Ó Cléirigh
joined the Franciscan community at Bundrowes, in
south Donegal, where they had taken refuge after being
driven from their friary at Donegal town. The Franciscan
friar settled into a routine of travelling from place to
place to copy manuscripts during the summer, and of
recopying the manuscripts at Bundrowes during the
winter. At the end of each transcript of a document, he
wrote a colophon saying where and when he had done

the work. By this means we can follow the learned friar's steps. In 1627 he was in Dublin, in Drogheda and in Kildare. In 1628 he followed "the track of the old books" to Athlone, Multyfarnham and Cashel. The next year he was at Limerick where he copied the *Miorbuile Senáin* (Miracles of St Senan). In the winter of 1630 he completed at Bundrowes his first great compilation, *Félire na naomh nErennach* (The Martyrology of Donegal) and sent it to Louvain. To complete the *Réim Rioghgraidhe* (1630), a list of the succession of the kings and the genealogies of the saints of Ireland, he had the help of three others, Fearfasa Ó Maolchonaire, Cucoigcriche Ó Duibhgheannain and Cucoigcriche Ó Cléirigh. Then all four began the compilation which made their names famous. The colophon records that "An dara lá fiche do mí Januarii anno Domini 1632 do tionnsgnadh an leabhar so i cconveint Dhúin na nGall..." By 1636 Brother Micheál and his helpers had finished a chronicle of the history of Ireland, from the time of the flood to the year 1608, which they called *Annála Rioghachta Éireann* (Annals of the Kingdom of Ireland), and which was later better known as the *Annals of the Four Masters*. Two copies were made, one for their patron Fergal Ó Gara, and the other for the college at Louvain. Ó Cléirigh himself may have taken the volume there for in July 1637 he left the Franciscan friary at Carrickfergus to sail for the Netherlands. He spent the rest of his life with his fellow Irish Franciscans at the Collège St Antoine in Louvain, working with John Colgan on the *Acta Sanctorum*, and producing a *Foclóir* of early Irish words. Micheál Ó Cléirigh OFM died at Louvain in 1643.

Peadar Ó Doirnín

?1704-69

The life of the seventeenth century poet, Peadar Ó
Doirnín, is shrouded in mystery and beset by controversy
and it seems unlikely now that even the main events of
his life will ever be clearly established. The Gaelic scholar,
Seán Ó Dálaigh claimed him as a Munster poet in his
Poets and Poetry of Munster (1849) and stated that he was
born in Cashel, Co Tipperary in 1704. However in a
memoir published in 1840, based, according to its own
claims, on the testimony of people who knew Ó Doirnín,
and written by Matthew Moore Graham, the birthplace
of Ó Doirnín is given as Ráth Sciathach (Risceagh), a
townland just north of Dundalk in Co Louth. The year of
his birth is stated to be 1704. There is a lesser level of
disagreement about the date of his death: it is variously
given as 1768 or 1769, but the earlier date seems the
result of a misreading of the official elegy written by his
fellow Ulster poet Art Mac Cumhthaigh. The young Ó
Doirnín seems to have received the extensive education,
especially in the classics, that was available to gifted
young men of his time, whether illegally as a Catholic—
one version of his life story has it that he was sent to
study for the priesthood—or under the tutelage of a local
Protestant minister, his mother being Protestant. In any
case, Ó Doirnín certainly seems to have been a Catholic
for all of his adult life—both his politics and his career
indicate this—and his mother is said to have died a
Catholic. He began to write poetry as a young man and

spent some years in Munster learning his trade and broadening his poetic horizons. On his return he began his career as a teacher, first in the house of a Mr Toner, whose daughter Rose he married. The couple are said to have had one child, a son, who did not inherit his father's intelligence. He also taught in the home of Arthur Brownlow of Lurgan, who was then in possession of the *Book of Armagh*, and made his employer familiar with the traditions of Gaelic literature. Teaching was a hazardous occupation for Catholics under the penal laws: one either tutored the household of a sympathetic Protestant or else became an itinerant schoolmaster for one's co-religionists. Ó Doirnín appears to have done both and to have taught in many different places in Co Louth and Co Armagh. He is said to have become involved with either the Whiteboys or the rapparees and to have taken part in the agrarian agitation that was so widespread and so vicious at the time. He certainly incurred the enmity of one Johnston "of the Fews" and was obliged to flee the area because of this. To add to the complexity of our picture of Ó Doirnín, he was also suspected of having betrayed a rapparee brother-in-arms who was subsequently hanged in Armagh—this, the story goes, is the reason for the lack of warmth of Art Mac Cumhaigh's elegy. He spent the last number of years of his life in a relatively stable and peaceful situation as teacher in Forkhill, Co Armagh. He died suddenly in his classroom there and was buried in Urney graveyard, north of Dundalk. He is best known today for his beautiful "Úrchnoc Chéin Mhic Cáinte." His output was not vast but was very varied, consisting of political and nature poetry, drinking stanzas and more personal verse.

Peadar O'Donnell

1893-1986

Peadar O'Donnell, the writer and social reformer, was born on 22 February 1893 at Meenmore, near Dungloe, Co Donegal not far from the birthplace twenty years earlier of another social reformer Paddy "The Cope" Gallagher*. Though conditions had improved somewhat because of the "Cope," life in the Rosses was still very hard. The young men and women went to the Laggan on hire or crossed to Scotland to do the rough farmwork at harvest time. O'Donnell's family was Larkinite and very conscious of social questions, especially the conditions under which the "tattie-howkers" were forced to live. Peadar became a teacher under the monitor scheme which finally won him entrance into St Patrick's Training College in 1910. The summer before he had made a trip to Scotland to see for himself what hardships the migrant workers had to suffer. Because of the strict regulations governing the life of the students O'Donnell saw little of Dublin, though the city was in ferment in those years with the kind of social upheaval that interested him. He was appointed to the school on Arranmore Island near his home and later taught on the smaller island of Inisfree. He left teaching after a brush with the inspectorate and became a full-time organiser for the Irish Transport and General Workers Union in 1918. He was active in the War of Independence, reaching the rank of commandant-general and, taking the anti-Treaty side in the civil war, was arrested when the Free State soldiers burned the Four Courts in June 1922. He was imprisoned in Mountjoy Gaol until his escape in 1924. During this time he had endured a hunger strike of forty-one days and was elected Sinn Féin TD for Donegal. In 1924 O'Donnell married Lile O'Donel, the daughter of a wealthy Connacht landlord who had been active with him in the socialist movement. While "on the run" in Donegal he became aware of the money that small farmers were required to pay under the Land Annuities scheme. The abolition of this iniquitous levy became his next cause, and so successfully did he prosecute it that the agitation helped bring down the Cosgrave government and paved the way for the "economic war". From 1926 to 1934 he edited *An Phoblacht*, the IRA journal and during the Spanish civil war organised opposition to Franco, collaborating with his old colleague Frank Ryan in recruiting for the International Brigade. In 1940 he persuaded Sean O'Faolain to edit *The Bell*, that clangorous monthly periodical that did so much to shake Ireland out of its provincial sleep and discover new voices to represent the country. When he took over as editor in 1946 it became more overtly political. Lile died in 1969 and Peadar survived her by seventeen years, dying on 13 May 1986. His writings, seven novels, three volumes of autobiography, much journalism and a play, are characteristic of the man's life. His great phrase which he used regularly was "a gait of going"—the way of living one's life. His was liberal and full of concern for the poor and the underprivileged. At no time was his radical voice stilled. He was refused a visa to visit USA because of his vocal socialism and he campaigned against nuclear armaments and American involvement in Vietnam, but he was no doctrinaire Marxist. His concern was for people and their need for idiosyncratic freedom. One of his most telling symbols occurs in the novel *The*

Big Windows (1954) in which the island woman Brigid married to a mountainy husband pines for the width of her island sky and finds comfort only when her husband builds her a house that lets in the same kind of light that she was used to. His finest novel is the spare *Islanders* (1927), a classic of island literature taking its inspiration from Arranmore and the other islands of the Rosses. His style was spare because he believed that language should do without ornamentation, and it was to the islands he returned for his final book *Proud Island* (1975) written when he was eighty-three. It is too a valediction for the practical reformer in him suggests that these picturesque rocky outcrops should never have been inhabited in the first place. They are a monument to social persecution. Better to give them back to the gannets. Throughout his ninety-three years of life Peadar O'Donnell fought for every cause whose supporters hoped to improve the human condition.

Tomás Ó Fiaich

1923-90

Cardinal-Archbishop of Armagh and primate of All Ireland, Tomás Ó Fiaich stood out in a rather colourless Catholic hierarchy, for his sociability and love of talking, for his enjoyment of appearing in public, for his pipe-smoking (also in public) and for his refusal to hide his nationalist sympathies. The first Armagh man to become primate since St Malachy in the twelfth century, Tomás Ó Fiaich was born at Cullyhanna near Crossmaglen on 3 November 1923, the younger son of Patrick Fee, a schoolteacher, and of a mother who died eight years after his birth. Ó Fiaich was educated at Cregganduff primary school, at St Patrick's College in Armagh, at Maynooth College (1940-44) and, after a year's break in studies due to pneumonia, at St Peter's College in Wexford. Ordained at Wexford for the archdiocese of Armagh on 6 June 1948, he became a post-graduate student at UCD where he took an MA in early Irish history (1950) and then at Louvain where he was awarded a *Licence-ès-sciences-historiques* for work on early Irish missionaries. A year as curate in the parish of Clonfeacle, on the Armagh-Tyrone border, followed before Ó Fiaich returned to academic life at Maynooth, as lecturer and then professor of modern history, as vice-president of the college (1970) and finally as president (1974). On 22 August 1977 he was the surprise choice of Rome to succeed Cardinal Conway at Armagh. Made a cardinal in the same year, Ó Fiaich welcomed John Paul II, the first

Pope ever to visit Ireland (September 1979). The papal visit was an event of great joy but much of Ó Fiaich's primacy was taken up with less happy matters, the divorce and abortion debates and the continuing political violence in Northern Ireland. It was on the latter that Ó Fiaich had particularly strong opinions, condemning IRA and other violence but also criticising British security policy. He was highly critical of British handling of the IRA prisoners' hunger strike (a hunger strike eventually brought to an end by the work of two priests of the Armagh archdiocese, Fathers Faul and Murray). For his criticism of British policy and for his openly declared nationalism, Ó Fiaich was the object of dislike of the British popular press and of many Northern unionists. On the other hand, many Protestants were attracted by his sociable personality and his genuine ecumenism. Ó Fiaich wrote both on history and on Irish and published, *inter alia*, *Irish Cultural Influence in Europe* (1967) and *Art MacCumhaigh* (1973), as well as editing *Seanchas Árd Mhacha*, the Armagh local history journal. But he took learning lightly and never was, nor wished to be, an intellectual heavyweight. Rather than a professional intellectual he was an amateur; of Art MacCumhaigh from his native south Armagh who wrote "Úrchill an Chreagáin"; of traditional music and Gaelic football; of the Irish language which he promoted by founding the Glór na nGael competition; of Ireland's ties with Germany and France, countries he loved and whose languages he spoke. Tomás Ó Fiaich died in a Toulouse hospital on 8 May 1990 after being taken ill while on pilgrimage to Lourdes. He was buried at Armagh amidst scenes of genuine popular grief for a man who, all agreed, had "the common touch."

Eoghan Rua O'Neill

c.1590-1649

A nephew of the great Hugh O'Neill (1550-1616)* and perhaps a more able soldier than his famous uncle, Eoghan Rua was the son of Art MacBaron O'Neill. Both he and his father were among the group of Gaelic nobles who felt it would be impossible to survive in an Ulster conquered and planted by Britain and so left for Spain (1607). Having trained as a soldier, Eoghan Rua served in the Spanish Netherlands in the long-drawn-out war against the French and the Dutch. By 1633 he had become colonel of O'Neill's Regiment in the Spanish army and in 1640 "Don Eugenio O'Neill" won fame all over Europe for his defence of Arras against a French siege. Meanwhile the state of affairs in Ireland was changed drastically by the outbreak of civil war in England and the victory of the puritan supporters of parliament over the more tolerant royalists. In Ireland the Gaelic Irish and the Old English came together to attempt to ease the severity of the Tudor religious and land settlements. O'Neill wrote that "In this hour of Ireland's troubles, I should not be absent or seem wanting." So, with two hundred veteran soldiers, he landed at Doe castle in Co Donegal (July 1642). By the "Assembly of Confederate Catholics of Ireland" which met in Kilkenny, O'Neill was appointed general for Ulster. He managed to prevent the Scottish parliamentarian army of Munro from controlling the province, and his victory at Benburb (5 June 1646) showed he was the most able of the Irish generals. But O'Neill was never given overall command because he supported the more radically Catholic policies of the Gaelic Irish (and of the papal nuncio, Rinuccini) against the less assertive ones of the Old English of Leinster; instead he was left to share command with Thomas Preston, a rival general who was less talented. In 1649 Rinuccini lost control of the confederacy and returned to Rome. This, and Cromwell's arrival in Ireland, left O'Neill with no alternative but to ally once more with the Old English and with the remaining Protestant royalists against the might of the parliamentarians, who were supported by most Irish Protestants. This alliance came too late both for Ireland and for O'Neill who died at Cloughoughter on 6 November 1649. He was mourned by his son Henry, soon afterwards beheaded, and by his wife Rosa O'Doherty, who returned to spend her widowhood in Brussels. O'Neill, with his belief that a common Catholicism was more important than differences of Irishness, was essentially an aristocrat imbued with the spirit of the later counter-reformation. His career is a reminder that Irish events in the seventeenth century were part of a European pattern, that of the Thirty Years' War.

Hugh O'Neill

1550-1616

The last great Gaelic prince, Hugh O'Neill, was born in 1550 at Dungannon. His family was forced to foster him to Sir Henry Sidney at Ludlow Castle and at Penshurst (1559-67). There he was reared to respect English culture and "the new religion." Returning to Ireland, he attempted, Janus-like, to be a peer subject to the English crown and to take control of the traditional *lucht tighe Uí Néill*. He led a troop of horse in helping the English put down the Desmond rebellion in 1569, and accepted the title of second Earl of Tyrone. But O'Neill never forgot that his basic strength lay in Gaelic Ulster and he acted accordingly, arranging the murder of a rival, Hugh Gavelock, and making a second marriage, to Red Hugh O'Donnell's sister, so as to cement an alliance with the Tír Conaill chieftain. Already in effective control of the lordship, Hugh O'Neill was inaugurated clan chieftain on Turlough Luineach's death in 1595. Unfortunately for O'Neill, he had antagonised the English military commander at Newry (by marrying his daughter, Mabel Bagenal, in 1591) and he had made the English officials in Dublin suspicious of him by his private communication with Philip II of Spain. He was declared a traitor and a succession of English commanders was sent to deal with him: Sir John Norris he defeated at Clontibret and Marshal Bagenal at the Yellow Ford (1598). Then O'Neill was faced with the might of the Earl of Essex and an army released from service in the Spanish Netherlands (after the death of Philip II) but he outwitted Elizabeth I's favourite and sent him home in disgrace. Now determined to become "Prince of Ireland" (under Spanish tutelage) O'Neill made a royal progress of both north and south while waiting for Spanish forces under Juan del Águila to arrive. But the 4,000 Spaniards landed at Kinsale, Co Cork, in December of 1601 and were surrounded by a new and able English commander, Lord Mountjoy, before O'Neill (accompanied by O'Donnell and others) could complete the long march from Ulster. When it arrived, O'Neill's army was unable to withstand the shock of attack from formed troops in the field, and after defeat he had to retire to Glanconcadhain in the clan heartland of Tyrone. Luckily for him, Mountjoy was in a hurry to return to the centre of power at court, and so he was allowed to submit at Mellifont (1603) while retaining all his powers over his old lordship. When a new group of English officials in Dublin used judicial means to reduce O'Neill's power, the Gaelic chieftain believed he could outwit them by using influence at the English royal court. But Maguire and O'Donnell decided to go into exile from Lough Swilly (September 1607) and, untypically, O'Neill panicked and joined them. After a long journey via Quillebeuf and Louvain, he arrived in Rome, to be given a house by the Pope and a pension by the Spanish. O'Neill continued to hope for a new Spanish invasion of Ireland, but in the end had to admit the success of the English policy of *"amistad fingida y de destruir con la paz"* (feigned friendship and peaceful conquest.) Survived by his fourth wife, and his son who became "*conde de Tirón*" in the Spanish aristocracy, Hugh O'Neill died on 20 July 1616 and was buried in the Franciscan church of San Pietro in Montorio. Though the original grave inscription was lost with the re-paving of the church in 1848, a succession of writers, from

Tadhg Ó Cianáin to Brian Friel, have kept alive the memory of one whom Seán Ó Faoláin saw as "the first step that his people made towards some sort of intellectual self-criticism as to their place and their responsibilities in the European system."

Terence O'Neill

1914-90

Even at his death, Terence O'Neill's name aroused conflicting emotions: Ken Whitaker, the Co Down Catholic who rose to be head of the civil service in Dublin, remembered a sensitive but charming man with "no side to him"; while Rev Ian Paisley refused the charity of his silence to the aristocrat he believed had destroyed unionist Ulster. Terence Marne O'Neill was born on 10 September 1914, the fifth child of the Honourable Arthur O'Neill, a Unionist MP for Mid-Antrim who was killed in the opening months of the 1914-18 war. His mother, a daughter of Lord Crewe, reared the family in London, but sent the children to Shane's Castle, Co Antrim on holidays. Her remarriage, to a British consul, brought the family to Addis Ababa. O'Neill was sent to Eton College and afterwards he spent a year abroad, learning both French and German. For a while he worked in the stock exchange and then went to South Australia as civilian aide-de-camp to the governor there. O'Neill joined the Irish Guards for the duration of the 1939-45 war and was with the Guards Armoured Division in Normandy, Belgium and the Netherlands (1944-5). By the time the war ended O'Neill was married, to Katherine Jean Whitaker, and had a son. "We wondered what to do with Terence and put him into politics," was how O'Neill's cousin Phelim remembered it: with his family, O'Neill moved to Ahoghill, Co Antrim, was chosen as Unionist candidate for Bannside (November

1946) and returned unopposed to parliament at Stormont. There he was a parliamentary secretary, from 1948, and a minister, briefly, of home affairs, and then of finance from September 1956. As minister he was responsible for setting up both the Ulster Museum and the Ulster Folk Museum. On 25 March 1963 he replaced Lord Brookeborough, who was old and ill, as Prime Minister. O'Neill decided that relationships with the Catholic minority and with the Dublin government could and should be improved. O'Neill's secretary, Jim Malley, arranged with Ken Whitaker, whom he had encountered at meetings of the World Bank, that Sean Lemass, the Taoiseach, should visit Stormont on 14 January 1965. At the same time O'Neill travelled all over the province, making a special point of being seen meeting Catholics. But many unionists opposed O'Neill's policy; discrimination in local government continued and a new university was established in unionist Coleraine rather than in majority-nationalist Derry. Younger, more radical nationalists protested against housing discrimination (at Caledon) and against unfair local government (in civil rights marches, the first at Derry on 5 October 1968). O'Neill, now under pressure from the government in London, made a number of reforms, including the abolition of Londonderry Corporation, with its unfairly-elected unionist majority. On 9 December 1968, he appeared on television, declaring that "Ulster was at the crossroads," and appealing for support for his policies. But unionists were deeply divided and O'Neill lost the support of three cabinet members, Faulkner*, Morgan and Craig. In the general election of February 1969, O'Neill failed to defeat those opposed to him in the Unionist party; indeed he himself came perilously close to defeat in Bannside at the hands of Rev Ian Paisley, then a radical young loyalist. Soon afterwards, on 1 May 1969, O'Neill was forced to hand over power to James Chichester-Clarke. In January 1970 he was made Lord O'Neill of the Maine and resigned from Stormont. In 1975 he moved permanently to Hampshire, completely disillusioned with the growing violence. He died there on 13 June 1990, survived by his wife, son and daughter. A shy, withdrawn but decent man, Terence O'Neill did not have the political ability to deal with those who opposed his policies.

Brian O'Nolan

1911-1966

Brian O'Nolan, the brilliant Irish satirist, novelist, dramatist and gadfly, was much better known by two of his many aliases, Flann O'Brien and Myles na Gopaleen. He was born in Strabane, Co Tyrone on 5 October 1911, the son of a customs official. The family later moved to Tullamore and finally settled in Dublin when his father was appointed to the customs service of the newly established Free State in 1922. Brian was educated in several Dublin schools before having a brilliant social career in UCD and leaving with an MA degree in Celtic Languages. He joined the civil service in 1935 and was appointed to the department of local government, where he remained until his retirement due to ill-health in 1953. His most famous work (as Flann O'Brien) was the breathtakingly complicated *At Swim-Two-Birds*. It was published in 1939 and was immediately made a cult, though its small print-run and the coming of the second World War made it a book less read than talked about. It was reissued with great success in 1959 and like all of the rest of his work is still in print. This recovery of his first novel led to a burst of literary activity and two other novels, *The Hard Life* (1961) and *The Dalkey Archive* (1964) followed. (A year after his death a novel, *The Third Policeman*, written in 1940 and not offered to any publisher, appeared, confirming his comic talent.) In 1941 he began writing a column called "Cruiskeen Lawn" for *The Irish Times*, a paper which under its editor,

R M Smyllie, was coming to terms with the new state and forgetting its British past. This began as a column in Irish but gradually more and more English crept in. It was signed "Myles na gCopaleen"and it became an Irish institution. Its scholarship, its satiric humour, its creation of mythic characters, including "His Satanic Majesty," "The Brother" and "Keats and Chapman," have made it a classic of modern Irish humour. It was as "Myles" that the literary civil servant became known to Dublin's equivalent of café society and it was this name that he used for *An Béal Bocht*, his glorious send-up of certain worshipful attitudes that the activists of the language revival had towards the wilder Gaelic-speaking parts of the Atlantic seaboard of Ireland. This was the name he subscribed to two plays, *Faustus Kelly* and *Thirst*. He died, not inappropriately, on 1 April 1966.

Dehra Parker
1882-1963

The only woman member ever of the Northern Ireland cabinet, Dehra Parker was born in 1882, the sole child of James Kerr-Fisher of Kilrea, Co Londonderry. After being educated privately, at the age of nineteen she married Robert Spencer Chichester of Castledawson, by whom she had a daughter. Widowed in 1921, she remarried in 1928, to Admiral HW Parker, but she was again a widow in 1940. Dehra Parker entered politics on the death of her first husband and was unionist MP for Derry City and County (1921-9). After a brief respite from politics when she remarried, she returned as MP for South Derry (one of the single-seat constituencies created after the abolition of proportional representation) in 1932, and continued to represent the same constituency until her retirement from Stormont in 1960. Dehra Parker showed herself to be an able politician. She argued for the abolition of PR, maintaining it was an MP's duty to represent all her constituents, and so nationalists could not be considered to have a grievance, even if they lost a seat under the new straight-vote system. She declared, high-mindedly, that "when we come to this house we do not come with the intention of submitting ourselves into the hands of the general public..."; but when she was visited by a deputation of local farmers she had the good political sense to change her mind about the 1935 Road and Railway Transport Bill. Her political ability was recognised in 1937 when she was made parliamentary secretary to the minister for education, Rev R Corkey, a Presbyterian clergyman. But she and her minister had conflicting temperaments and she did not really mind having to resign in 1944, when Basil Brooke* replaced Corkey with Hall-Thompson. In 1949 when she was made Dame, Dehra Parker became minister for health and local government, an office she held until 1957. At the same time she was president of the Council for the Encouragement of Music and the Arts (1949-60). She was immensely influential in unionist politics and ensured that when she resigned in 1960, her seat was won by her grandson, Major James Chichester-Clark. The story is also told that she directed that Terence O'Neill*, to whom she was related, should succeed Brookeborough as premier and that he in turn should be followed by Chichester-Clarke (which was exactly what happened). Dehra Parker continued to live in Castledawson, where she fished for relaxation, until her death on 28 November 1963.

Saidie Patterson

1906-85

Linen weaver, trade unionist, peacemaker and above all, a Christian in the Methodist tradition, Saidie Patterson was born on 25 November 1906 in the house where she spent all her life, at 32 Woodvale Street, off the Shankill Road in Belfast. She was one of three children of William Patterson, a shipyard blacksmith, and of Sarah whom he had met while worshipping at the Methodist Grosvenor Hall. When Saidie's father died, aged twenty-seven, her mother married Thomas Gracey, a widower with five young children. He was afterwards stricken with a nervous disease which left him unable to work; so Saidie and seven other children depended on her mother's earnings as an outworker, which averaged eighty pence for making up five hundred linen sheets. Saidie's only education was at Woodvale National School in Cambrai Street in a class of more than fifty and with a supply of charity books. In 1918 she saw her mother die in childbirth since the family was unable to afford a doctor. Soon afterwards Saidie became an apprentice weaver in Ewart's linen factory on the Crumlin Road. There she won the backing of the whole mill for her refusal to apologise to a foreman she had attacked physically when he berated a sick factory girl for sitting down. Her charisma saved her but Saidie realised that a lesser woman would have lost her job at a time when women workers were not organised in trade unions. Under the influence of Bob Getgood and Ernest Bevin of the Amalgamated Transport and General

Workers Union, she organised the women workers of Ewart's and after a seven-week strike in 1940 the union won an increase in pay and holidays with pay. In the same year Saidie became a full-time official of the union. Union involvement led naturally to an interest in the Northern Ireland Labour Party which she helped revive in 1938. In 1945 she worked hard to have Bob Getgood returned to Stormont for North Belfast. As chairman she led the party to win four seats in the 1958 election, on a platform of "bridge-building inside Northern Ireland and between North and South." At this period Saidie was strongly influenced by Frank Buchman's Moral Re-Armament crusade; she visited him at Caux in Switzerland and thought his belief, that personal reform led to reform of society, a modern restatement of Wesley's teaching. The political breakdown in Northern Ireland in the late 1960s allowed Saidie give practical expression to her beliefs; she became chairperson of Women Together, the movement founded in 1970 by Ruth Agnew to allow women more say in a province torn by strife. Believing "we don't need a gun in our hand; what we need is an idea in our heads and an answer in our hearts," she helped Máiréad Corrigan and Betty Williams organise a peace-march of 50,000 women up the Shankill Road, and welcomed them in Woodvale Park "not as Protestants or Catholics but as children of the King of Kings"(28 August 1976). Such dangerously Christian language led to the stoning of a follow-up march on the Falls Road and to a spell in hospital for Saidie Patterson. But she refused to compromise her beliefs; in September 1979 she was among those who travelled to Dublin to welcome the first Pope ever to visit Ireland and was invited to address an ecumenical peace vigil at St Patrick's Cathedral on the eve of the visit. Saidie's uniqueness was marked by a number of awards: the Joseph Parker Peace

Prize; the World Methodist Peace Award (at the reception in Geneva she heard that her nephew had been killed by the IRA); an Open University honorary degree; above all by being chosen as one of the fifty most distinguished women in the world by the Geneva committee which organised the International Women's Year in 1975. She died in 1985.

William Pirrie
1847-1924

The man who made Harland and Wolff "shipbuilders to the world" was born on 24 May 1847 in Quebec, where his father, James Pirrie from Co Down, had gone to learn the timber business. When Pirrie's father died in 1849 his mother, Eliza Swan Montgomery, took him home to Ireland. He grew up at Conlig, Co Down, in the house of his grandfather, William Pirrie, who was a shipping merchant in Belfast. Pirrie attended the Royal Belfast Academical Institution from 1858 and in 1862 became a shipbuilder's apprentice at Harland and Wolff's yard. There he rose quickly and by 1874 was chief draughtsman and a partner. In the 1880s the founding partners, Edward Harland and Gustav Wolff, were no longer actively involved and Pirrie was the most powerful man in the company. In 1879 Pirrie married his beautiful and intelligent cousin, Margaret Montgomery Carlisle. They bought Ormiston, Harland's house at Castlereagh, on the outskirts of Belfast, and Pirrie became chairman of the company on Harland's death in 1895. Mayor of Belfast in 1896, he was made the city's first freeman at the end of his term of office. In 1899 Harland and Wolff built the *Oceanic* for the White Star Line; at 17,000 tons she was the largest ship afloat. Pirrie had become the world's leading shipbuilder and an immensely powerful businessman: he had an agreement to build for J Pierpoint Morgan, the American railway millionaire; he and partner Owen Philipps controlled the Union Castle fleet of forty-four ships; he was collaborating with Burmeister and Wain of Denmark to produce marine diesel engines in the UK; his company, Harland and Wolff, now had yards at Govan, Liverpool, Southampton and London, as well as at Belfast. In 1900 the Pirries moved to Downshire House in London and they bought a country house at Witley Court in Surrey. There they entertained magnificently but felt they were not accepted by London society. In politics too Pirrie was an outsider. His Non-Subscribing Presbyterianism made him a natural liberal and cost him a nomination for the South Belfast seat in the 1902 election. Because of his support of liberal candidates in the 1906 election he was knighted. He supported limited devolution for Ireland and in 1912 chaired a meeting in Celtic Park, Belfast, at which John Redmond and Winston Churchill spoke in favour of Home Rule. But by the same year 1912, Pirrie had aged as a result of illness, had lost his designer Thomas Andrews in the *Titanic* tragedy, and was concealing, even from his chief accountant, the fact that the company was heavily overdrawn. The 1914-18 war came to his relief: Harland and Wolff became a "controlled establishment" producing warships, cargo ships and planes for the ministry of munitions; Pirrie became controller-general of merchant shipbuilding, raising the output of standard ships by fifty per cent in 1918. Immediately after the war there was a shipbuilding boom, followed by a collapse in 1920. At the same time, the "troubles", which both caused (and were caused by) the setting up of Northern Ireland, reached their height. Pirrie dealt with the resultant sectarian and trade union difficulties in the shipyard pragmatically. But he had now become conservative; he was made a member of the new Northern Ireland senate and a viscount in 1922. And he had become an autocrat surrounded by managers who did not dare question his running of the ailing firm of Harland and Wolff. Pirrie died of pneumonia on board the *Ebro* (7 June 1924) while on a cruise to South America, leaving Lord Kylsant, his successor at Harland and Wolff, with an almost bankrupt company and a bitter enemy in Lady Pirrie, who resented inevitable criticism of her husband's running of the firm. The greatest Irish businessman of his day, Pirrie epitomised hard-headed Belfast, proud of its industrial competence and competing on a world market.

Oliver Plunkett

1625-81

Old English, Roman academic, Archbishop of Armagh, martyr, canonised saint, Oliver Plunkett was born on 1 November 1625 at Loughcrew, near Oldcastle, Co Meath. He was the son of John Plunkett, Baron of Loughcrew, and of Thomasina Dillon. Influenced by his first teacher, Patrick Plunkett, who was the parish priest of Kilcloon and a cousin of his mother, Oliver Plunkett journeyed to Rome in 1647 to study philosophy and theology at the Irish College. After his ordination in 1654 he begged not to be sent back to Cromwellian war-torn Ireland, but instead to be allowed study canon and civil law. His wish was granted and he became a professor of theology at Propaganda College in 1657. There he acquired both his belief that "the man educated in Rome has the knowledge and the ability to govern," and the fluent Italian which allowed him to communicate so ably with Cardinal Baldeschi of Propaganda, later on. In 1669 Pope Clement IX, rejecting the list of three names sent from Ireland, chose Plunkett as Archbishop of Armagh. He returned, via Ghent where he was consecrated, to Ireland, there to be welcomed warmly by his English-speaking kinsmen of the Pale, less warmly by the Gaelic clergy of the greater part of the archdiocese of Armagh. The outsider from Meath set to work to enforce the new ideals of the Roman counter-reformation. He insisted that the clergy should lead blameless lives, free of drunkenness and concubinage. He brought Jesuits in to the diocese to open schools. He adjudicated against the Franciscans in a dispute with the Dominicans about the ownership of three friaries. He wrote *Ius Primatiale* (1672) to justify his primacy, as Archbishop of Armagh, over Archbishop Peter Talbot of Dublin. Above all he travelled all over Ulster, regulating the clergy, confirming the faithful. And he reported on his work, in a loyal and voluminous correspondence with Rome. Of course, Plunkett ministered in a land which was officially Protestant and so he worked circumspectly, relying on his friends in the Dublin administration and in the Protestant hierarchy to secure him toleration. This lasted until 1678, when England, under the influence of Titus Oates's concocted story about a "popish plot," was swept by an anti-Catholic frenzy. The administration in Ireland was forced to arrest the Archbishop of Dublin and Plunkett went into hiding. In 1679 Plunkett was arrested and lodged in Dublin Castle on a charge of plotting a French invasion. His trial opened at Dundalk where the two disaffected clergymen who were to witness against him, Murphy and McMoyer, were too ashamed to give evidence they knew was false. The trial was moved to London where Plunkett, unable to call defence witnesses from Ireland, was found guilty by a jury imbued with the prevailing spirit. After having, according to a fellow prisoner, "spent his time in almost continuous prayer," Plunkett was brought to Tyburn to be executed on 1 July 1681. Declaring that an Irish Protestant jury would no more have believed the charges against him than they would have believed he "had flown in the air from Dublin to Holyhead," he died, the last man to be martyred for the Catholic faith in England.

Robert Lloyd Praeger

1865-1953

Born in August 1865 at Hollywood, Co Down, the son of Willem Praeger, a Dutch linen merchant, and of Maria (daughter of Robert Patterson, the celebrated Belfast naturalist), RL Praeger was educated at Royal Belfast Academical Institution and Queen's College Belfast. As a young man he was intensely interested in geology and he wrote many papers on Irish quaternary geology. At first a civil engineer in the Belfast water service, he then joined the staff of the National Library in Dublin (1893), where he became chief librarian in 1920 before retiring in 1924. Retirement allowed him give all his time to his great interest in natural history, an interest begun in the Belfast Naturalist's Field Club and continued in the Dublin Field Club. He was in turn president of the RIA (1931), the Geographical Society of Ireland (1937), the Royal Horticultural Society of Ireland (1949-50) and of the Royal Zoological Society of Ireland. He wrote profusely on the environment, as editor of the *Irish Naturalist*, (which he helped found) and in his books: *Flora of the County Armagh* (1893), *The Botanist in Ireland* (1934), *The Natural History of Ireland* (1950) and *The Way that I Went* (1937). This last volume gives a vivid picture of a man and his place. The opening sentence reads: "The way that I went was an Irish way, with extraorbital aberrations, especially in the later years, to the extent of a thousand or maybe fifteen hundred miles. It was from the beginning a way of flowers and stones and beasts." Praeger thought

Ireland "a very lovely country" but regretted "…that the people who are in it have not the common-sense to live in peace with one another and with their neighbours." He felt that Ireland had brought the partition on herself but he retained an abiding love of his country: "I have wandered about Europe from Lapland to the Aegean Sea…but I have always returned with fresh appreciation of my own land. I think that is as it should be." He had married Hedwig Magnusson of Schleswig in 1902. He died in Belfast on 5 May 1953.

Amanda McKittrick Ros

1860-1939

Amanda McKittrick, "the worst novelist in the world," was born in Drumaness, near Ballynahinch, Co Down in 1860. She was the fourth child of a local headmaster and of solidly respectable Presbyterian stock. Her tendency towards romantic attitudes and her lush literary style are due in part to a fondness for the popular novels of Marie Corelli, but most of it was temperamental. She claimed that the McKittricks were descended from Sitric the "King of the Danes," and on such flimsy evidence claimed kinship with Danish royalty. She was a student at Marlborough Street teachers' college when she met her husband, Andy Ross, the stationmaster of Larne, Co Antrim, the port of embarkation for Scotland by the short sea-route. Andy was thirty-five years to her twenty and a tolerant man. He did not object when she insisted after the wedding that her name in full was Amanda Malvina Fitzalan Anna Margaret McLelland McKittrick Ros. Her first novel, *Irene Iddesleigh,* she published at her own expense in 1897. (She never had much time for publishers; she once wrote in a letter: "I consider they're too grabby altogether. They love to keep the Sabbath and everything else they lay their hands on.") Her literary style was florid and at times uncontrolled: Lord Redfern of Redfern, the hero of *Irene Iddesleigh,* is described as one "[who] never yet had entertained the thought of yielding up his bacheloric ideas to supplace them with others which eventually should coincide with those of a different sex." She became in her lifetime a kind of cult among the bookmen of the time. Desmond MacCarthy, E V Lucas and F Anstey used meet to read excerpts from her later novels, *Delina Delaney, Donald Dudley* and *Helen Huddlestone* (alliteration was one of her favourite devices). She never realised that Aldous Huxley's promotion of the novels which led to their being republished was based on anything other than genuine appreciation of them as literature. She also wrote volumes of verse with (again) alliterative titles : *Poems of Puncture* and *Fumes of Formation.* Her "Lines on Westminster Abbey" show the remarkable eccentricity of her language and her capacity for olympian bathos:

Holy Moses! Have a look!
Flesh decayed in every nook.
Some rare bits of brain lie here,
Mortal loads of beef and beer...

Andy Ross died in 1917 and nine years later she married a farmer called Rogers. She died in February 1939 to become herself "a litter of worms, a relic of humanity."

Charles Russell

1832-1900

An Irish Catholic who became Lord Chief Justice of England, Charles was the son of Arthur Russell, a Newry ship and brewery owner, and of Margaret Hamill (née Mullan) of Belfast. Born at Ballybot, Newry, on 10 November 1832 into a very religious family (an uncle was president of Maynooth college, all four sisters became Mercy nuns, and an only brother a Jesuit), Russell was educated at St Malachy's, Belfast and at St Vincent's, Castleknock, Dublin. He was an apprentice solicitor at Newry and Belfast (1848-54) before making a name for his defence of Cushendall Catholics charged with assaulting Protestant missionaries. Russell studied law at TCD and Lincoln's Inn, from where he was called to the English bar (in preference to the Irish where the northern circuit especially, was Protestant dominated). Russell worked as a barrister in Liverpool and the north of England, where, though neither a great lawman nor an orator, he impressed juries with his bluntness and his great physical presence. After two unsuccessful attempts, he was elected Liberal MP for Dundalk (1880) and later, on the abolition of his borough constituency, MP for Hackney (1885-94). Russell had been a youthful admirer of John Mitchel and he remained a nationalist who believed in Irish self-government. But he also came to believe in the greatness of the British empire and the part Irishmen played in ruling it. Attorney-General for England under Gladstone (1886 and 1892), he showed his skills as advocate in the Bering Sea arbitration. But his greatest triumph was when he showed that the letters published by *The Times*, implicating Parnell in condonation of the murder of Chief Secretary Cavendish and his under-secretary, Burke, by assassins in the Phoenix Park, had been forged by Richard Pigott (proved by Pigott's inability to spell "hesitancy"). In 1894 Gladstone made Russell Lord of Appeal and in 1895 Lord Chief Justice (being unable to bestow the chancellorship on him as a Catholic). As Lord Chief Justice, Russell of Killowen was able and efficient but was not long enough in office to make a lasting impact. He died in London on 10 August 1900, fortified by the rites of the church he loved, in the company of his wife (Ellen Mulholland from Belfast whom he had married in 1858) and of his numerous children.

George William Russell (Æ)

1867-1937

The man who once described a literary movement as "four or five people who live in the same town and hate each other," was born in Lurgan, Co Armagh, on 10 April 1867, the son of a book-keeper. The family moved to Dublin in 1878 but Russell's Ulster origin was not forgotten, as his ironic description, by the elder Yeats, as "a saint—but born in Portadown" indicates. He was educated at Rathmines School and later became a clerk in Pim's drapery store in South Great George's Street. He was interested in painting and enrolled in night classes at the Metropolitan School of Art and later at the Royal Hibernian Academy. Here he met W B Yeats who became one of his closest friends. He was attracted to mysticism and became a Theosophist in 1890. In 1894 he met Sir Horace Plunkett and joined him in helping to run the Irish Agricultural Organisation Society (IAOS). For eight years he toured Ireland, helping to establish credit banks as the basis for the security of the agricultural cooperative. In 1905 he became editor of the IAOS organ *The Irish Homestead*. In spite of much travel and editorial work he still found time to paint, write poetry and, on 11 June 1898, marry Violet North, a fellow adept. He also contributed a play, *Deirdre*, to the Irish Literary Theatre which his friend Yeats and Lady Gregory had founded and designed posters and painted sets. In the *Homestead* he supported all Irish aspirations, including Home Rule and the workers' cause during the 1913 lock-out. The

1916 rising took him by surprise, as it did many, and though as a pacifist he deplored the resort to violence he had great admiration for the courage of the men who died for their convictions. He organised a subscription for James Connolly's widow and tried to get permission for her to go to America. He was greatly distressed by the civil war and found the Free State oppressive and narrow-minded. There is a story that at the time of the Eucharistic Congress held in Dublin in 1932 he was seen standing on a rock at Glengarriff calling down a thunderstorm upon the "damned Christian idolaters" who were at their devotions in Phoenix Park. His work as editor of the *Irish Statesman* (1923-30) provided a literary outlet in what seemed to have become a culturally barren country. His house in Rathgar Avenue was a meeting place for all who held that art and economics were equally essential to the future of the new nation. When his wife died in 1932 he found life in Ireland very lonely. He left for England and lived in London. He developed cancer and died in a Bournemouth nursing home on 17 July 1935. As mystic, visionary, poet, painter and shaper of modern Ireland he well deserved the description by Archbishop Gregg, "that myriad-minded man."

Philip Sheridan
1831-88

Philip Henry Sheridan, the Union general, was born on 6 March 1831 at Killinkere, Co Cavan and taken to America at a very early age. His family settled at Somerset in Perry county, Ohio. Young Sheridan was sent to West Point, the US Military Academy, in 1848 but his graduation was deferred for a year because he struck a cadet sergeant. In 1853 he was sent west and saw service in Oregon, California and in Washington Territory. By 1861 he was a full lieutenant and he was soon promoted to captain. He came to the notice of General Halleck because of his bureaucratic skills and when the Civil War began he was chief quartermaster of the Union Army of southwest Missouri. He had yet to demonstrate military skill and it looked at one stage as if he would sit out the war as a non-combatant. On 25 May 1862, however, he took command of the Second Michigan Volunteer Cavalry Regiment (a position secured for him by a friend in Washington DC) and on 1 July defeated a greatly superior Confederate force at Boone, Missouri. Phil Sheridan had found his métier at last. He was to distinguish himself as an infantry commander before he was given his head as a cavalry general and became the main architect of the defeat of Confederate commander-in-chief, Robert E Lee. He won the battles of Parryville and Stone's River in the same busy year of 1862 and to crown his achievements was made major-general on 31 December. He fought with great distinction at Missionary Ridge, Chattanooga, the following November and in April 1864 was appointed cavalry commander of the Army of the Potomac by General Grant, the leader of the Union forces, again on the recommendation of his old mentor Halleck. His hard-riding campaign in the Shenandoah valley in the summer and autumn of 1864 replicated the swathe cut by General Sherman through Georgia. The same kind of swift campaign in the spring of the following year cut off Lee's line of retreat to Richmond. Sheridan won the last great battle of the war at Five Forks, Virginia, on 1 April 1865 and his continuing harassment of Lee's retreating forces forced the surrender of the Confederates at Appomattox on 9 April. After the war Sheridan was sent to subdue Texas and proved so stern as military governor that President Johnson, Lincoln's successor, had to withdraw him in 1867. He was promoted to the rank of lieutenant-general in 1869 and accompanied the Prussian Army as observer during the Franco-Prussian war of 1870. In 1883 he succeeded Sherman as commander-in-chief of the army. He was promoted to the rank of general shortly before his death at Nonquitt, Massachusetts, on 5 August 1888. Sheridan had great personal magnetism in spite of his reputation as a strict, even harsh, disciplinarian and was essentially a "modern" general with a grasp of administrative skills and a proper appreciation of situations reports.

Sir Hans Sloane

1660-1753

Hans Sloane, the physician and naturalist who founded the British Museum, was born in Killyleagh, Co Down on 16 April 1660. He was the son of Alexander Sloane the tax-collector and protégé of James Hamilton, the 1st Viscount of Clandeboye, who had received the grant of land from James I. He was the youngest of seven sons and his youth was spent roaming the shores of Strangford Lough and developing the interest in botany and zoology that marked his maturity. At sixteen he developed tuberculosis and determined to fight it by leading a moderate life. He was successful in that he did not die until his ninety-third year. He went to London in 1679, to the enlightened city of Wren, Pepys, Evelyn and Boyle, and studied medicine there and later in Paris, finally graduating as a Doctor of Physick from the University of Orange in 1683. In 1685 he became a member of the Royal Society and 1687 saw his election as an FRCP. That same year he sailed to Jamaica, almost certainly to avoid involvement in the coming clash between James II and the Whigs. While there he collected a herbarium of 800 plants. He returned to the London of William and Mary and established a fashionable medical practice in Bloomsbury. In 1695 he married a young widow, Elizabeth Rose, who brought Sloane a step-daughter and bore him four more children, two of whom died in infancy. His interest in science and in collecting books and plants never wavered. He attended Queen

Anne at her death and remained an unofficial royal doctor until his appointment as King's Physician to George II in 1727. He had been made a baronet in 1716. Throughout his long life he maintained his interest in natural history. His major work, which was published in two volumes in 1707 and 1727, was the *Natural History of Jamaica*. He was visited by the great equivalents from other countries, delighting in Linnaeus the great Swedish botanist and in Benjamin Franklin from whom he bought an asbestos purse. His collection of some 50,000 books, 3500 manuscripts and many specimen cases went to form the nucleus of the British Museum which was opened in Bloomsbury not far from his home in 1759, six years after his death. His family received £20,000 for the material. Sloane died on 11 January 1753.

Robert Stewart, Lord Castlereagh

1769-1822

Remembered in Britain as a great foreign secretary, in Ireland as the architect of an Act of Union which did not last, Robert Stewart (Viscount Castlereagh, after his father became Earl of Londonderry in 1796) was born to Robert Stewart and Sarah (née Seymour-Conway) in Dublin on 18 June 1769. After the early death of his mother, he was reared by his grandparents at Mountstewart near Newtownards, and then by his stepmother, a daughter of Lord Camden. He was educated at Armagh Royal School and at St John's College Cambridge (where, though an able classicist, he did not finish his degree). Attracted both by Irish and British politics, he became "patriot" (or opposition) MP for Co Down in 1790 when his father went to the House of Lords and, under the influence of his step-grandfather Camden, in 1794 a supporter of William Pitt, as MP for a Cornish borough. He saw service with the militia against the United Irishmen before becoming Chief Secretary to the Lord Lieutenant (his uncle, Lord Camden, appointed him, but Lord Cornwallis kept him on because he was "so unlike an Irishman" as to be suitable for a job traditionally filled by an Englishman). It was Castlereagh's skilful use of the necessary bribery which allowed Cornwallis to bring about the union of the Irish with the British parliament in 1800. When the Union did not bring emancipation for the Catholics, which Castlereagh had hoped for, he resigned, but was soon back in office as president of the India Board (1802). War secretary at a time when Napoleon seemed invincible, Castlereagh could do little save reorganise the army for Wellington's later triumphs. Made to resign against his will, he fought a duel with Canning over the matter. Out of office, Castlereagh lived happily with his wife Lady Emily (née Hobart) at North Cray, Kent, where he farmed sheep. Returned to office in the government reshuffle of 1812, as Foreign Secretary (1812-22) he was the principal actor, after Metternich, in the peace negotiations which led to the treaty of Vienna (1815). Later, he had less influence in the European "concert" because of a British policy of minimum involvement. On 12 August 1822 at North Cray, Castlereagh cut his throat while suffering from severe psychotic depression, brought on by the death of his father a year earlier (and perhaps because he was being blackmailed after being sexually compromised by a "woman" who turned out to be a man). He was buried, appropriately for the architect of the Union, at Westminster Abbey.

William Thomson, Baron Kelvin

1824-1907

William Thomson, the scientist and inventor, was born in College Square East, Belfast on 26 June 1824. His father, James Thomson, was professor of mathematics in the Royal Belfast Academical Institution which in the days before the establishment of the Queen's Colleges had quasi-university status. In 1832 his father was appointed professor of mathematics at Glasgow University and two years later the gifted son matriculated at the age of eleven. Thomson became an undergraduate of Peterhouse, Cambridge in 1841 when he was seventeen and graduated four years later. His genius was recognised early and he had already begun to make his mark when he was appointed to the chair of natural philosophy in Glasgow in 1846. He held the chair for fifty-three years and by the time he came to retire he was entitled to write more academic honours after his name than any man then alive. (During his life he was twice elected a fellow of Peterhouse: 1846-52 and 1872-1907.) He was not nor never became the stereotype scholar with purely academic preoccupations. He was a champion rower at Cambridge and one of the founders of the university Music Society. He remained a keen and effective yachtsman all his life and was so clever with his hands that he made his own prototypes for his many inventions. Under him Glasgow became a powerhouse of scientific research. His main claim to fame was his enunciation between 1851 and 1854 to the Royal Society of Edinburgh of the two great laws of thermodynamics which deal with the equivalence and capacity for transformation, one to the other, of heat and work. For this research on energy he was elected a Fellow of the Royal Society in 1851. Throughout his long and productive life Thomson insisted on the practical application of scientific discovery to utilitarian ends. His work on electric oscillations formed the basis of wireless telegraphy and in 1854, the year after his statement of the oscillation theory, he had invented a workable telegraph cable. In 1858 with typical practicality he served as electrician on the *Agamemnon*, the first ship to attempt to lay cable across the Atlantic, and had to stand by while a senior colleague ruined the success of the project by ignoring his instructions. Eight years later he succeeded triumphantly in laying a cable and was knighted in tribute. The catalogue of his theories, discoveries and inventions reads like a history of nineteenth-century electrical engineering. He worked on atmospheric electricity, the theory of elasticity and gyrostatics; he improved the mariner's compass, devised an apparatus to take accurate soundings and a machine for predicting tides, and demonstrated the principle of hydro-electricity using Niagara as an example. He campaigned vigorously for the standardisation of scientific units and in tribute to him the name, Kelvin of Largs, which he adopted in 1892 on his elevation to a barony, became the standard of temperature measurement under the modern Système International d'Unités (1 kelvin=9/5 degrees Fahrenheit) He was married twice, to Margaret Crum, his second cousin, in 1852, and four years after her death in 1870, to Frances Anna Blandy. In 1896 the golden jubilee of his professorship was attended by scientists from all over the world and an exhibition of his many inventions was held as part of the jubilee celebrations. In 1902 he was created a Privy Councillor and was one of the first to be granted the new Order of Merit. He died on 17 December 1907 at his mansion at Netherall near Largs on the west coast of Scotland and was buried in Westminster Abbey on 23 December. He was an ardent unionist in politics and strongly religious throughout his life. In his later years he became rather rigid in his attitudes, rejecting such advances in physics as radioactivity and X-rays.

John Toland
1670-1722

John Toland, deist, philosopher, pamphleteer, secular
and biblical scholar and linguist, was born near
Clonmany, Co Donegal on 30 November 1670. His
parentage is uncertain, but he was a Catholic and a
Gaelic-speaker and became a Protestant at sixteen. He
was educated at a hedge-school at Redcastle in the same
county and took his MA degree at Glasgow in 1690. After
a period of research at Leyden in Holland and a time at
Oxford (where he had the reputation of being "a man of
fine parts, great learning and little religion") he
abandoned his intention of becoming a dissenting
minister. He eventually moved to London where, apart
from a number of journeys to the continent and one
brief visit to Dublin, he spent the remainder of his days.
In 1696 Toland published *Christianity Not Mysterious*, a
book which gained him instant fame and which began
the conflict between those who, following Toland, called
themselves "deists" and orthodox believers. Toland,
while claiming to accept all the essentials of Christianity,
set out to show that it was a rational religion. He argued
that an event or doctrine could be called "mysterious" if
on analysis it is found to contain a contradiction. If
Christianity contained such doctrines then no reasonable
man could be asked to accept it. There should be no
conflict between reason and revelation. Faith requires
both knowledge and assent and is of no avail without the
confirmation of reason. He questioned the authority of

the Bible as a basis for belief and affirmed that "priestcraft" introduced "mysteries" and then fostered them by ceremonies and discipline. Reaction to the book was predictable. It was burned by the common hangman on the order of Parliament as "atheistic and subversive" and when Toland made a brief visit to Dublin in 1697 he was forced to fly the country. His subsequent career was disorganised. He made a kind of living as a writer of political pamphlets and he continued his tractical drive against orthodoxy. He wrote a life of John Milton and in *Letters to Serena* he produced a treatise on the philosophical basis of motion. He became more and more extreme in his rationalism and eventually embraced Pantheism, a term he coined in 1705. His works were translated into French and German and they proved to be very influential. He was regarded as a precursor of the Age of Reason. He died in poverty at Putney, near London, on 11 March 1722.

Helen Waddell

1889-1965

Helen Waddell, the medieval scholar, dramatist and novelist, was born in Tokyo on 31 May 1889, the youngest of ten children of Hugh Waddell, a Presbyterian missionary from Belfast. Her mother died of typhoid when she was almost three. The family had returned to Belfast when the mother fell ill but Hugh was not given permission to accompany them. When he did arrive back home he found that his wife was dead and buried and that his youngest daughter was dying of the same malady. He roused her out of a coma by speaking sharply to her in Japanese. In 1893 he married his cousin Martha Waddell and settled in Belfast. It was then a city not without culture and would soon take pride in its Ulster Literary Theatre, for which one of his sons, Samuel, as Rutherford Mayne, wrote its two most famous plays, *The Drone* and *The Turn of the Road*. Hugh died on 20 June 1901, when Helen was twelve, but she was able to continue her education at Victoria College and later at the Queen's University of Belfast, as Queen's College became in 1908. For a while she hesitated between Mathematics and English, being equally proficient in these seemingly contrasted subjects, but it was in English that she took her First in 1911. She wrote her MA thesis on "John Milton as Epicurist" and was awarded the Isabella Tod Memorial Scholarship. By now her stepmother was an invalid and an alcoholic, and for ten years Helen was unable to continue her academic career because of the need to nurse her pathologically strict and often ungrateful charge. During this enforced domestic exile she published *Lyrics from the Chinese* in 1915 and had a play, *The Spoilt Buddha*, performed by the Ulster players at the Opera House that same year. Martha Waddell died on 25 June 1920 and Helen was at last free to resume her studies. She went to Somerville College, Oxford to do research for her PhD on the secular origins of the stage. The "Fuff-Dee," as she called it, was never written but out of her researches into medieval literature came the books which made her famous; she was an even better Latinist than a mathematician. She published *The Wandering Scholars* in 1927 and *Medieval Latin Lyrics* in 1929. It was her novel *Peter Abelard* (1933) which made her name known outside of academe. It has been republished many times and is reckoned to have been the most popular historical novel ever written. Several more books followed, including *The Desert Fathers* (1936), and she continued a career of lecturing, broadcasting and literary journalism. From the late forties Helen Waddell suffered from progressive failure of the brain which manifested itself first as amnesia and later led to extinction of her personality. She died of pneumonia on 5 March 1965, having been completely incapacitated for ten years.

William Whitla

1851-1933

The first illustrious member of Belfast's young medical
school, William Whitla was born in Monaghan on 15
September 1851. The fourth son of Robert Whitla, a
woollen draper who had married Anne Williams of
Dublin, he was educated at the Model School, Monaghan
and then apprenticed to the Belfast chemist's firm of
Wheeler and Whitaker. Whitla went on to Queen's
College, Belfast where he took a first class honours
medical degree and won a gold medal (1872-7). He
became consultant physician to the Royal Victoria Hospital, Belfast and, in 1890, professor of *materia medica* at
his old college. He was elected president of both the
Ulster Medical Society and of the Irish Medical Association. The prominent part he played in the British
Medical Association meeting in Dublin (1887) and at the
International Congress of Medicine at Rome (1894)
brought him recognition from the outside medical world.
Knighted in 1902, he was president of the BMA in 1909
when its annual meeting was held in Belfast, and he was
also honoured by universities in Dublin, Glasgow and
Palermo. Whitla played a major part in the life of what
had become Queen's University, Belfast, being first MP
for the university, 1918-23, and pro-vice-chancellor,
1924. He married Ada Bourne from Stafford but the
marriage was childless. Whitla's interests extended
beyond the world of medicine: he was president of the
Belfast Young Men's Christian Association, and he was a

member of the Irish Convention which failed to secure nationalist-unionist agreement on the future government of the country in 1917-18. Whitla died in Belfast on 11 December 1933, after a long illness. He is remembered in medical history as an early supporter of Léon Calmette's theory that TB was caught via the intestines rather than by inhalation; and was the author of three long-lived textbooks, *Elements of Pharmacy, Materia Medica and Therapeutics* (1882), *Manual of Practice and Theory of Medicine* (1908), and a *Dictionary of Treatment* (1891). That the last-named volume ran to seven editions in English and to six in Chinese gives some indication of the stature of William Whitla in the medical world of his day.